s✝ill

By Dawn Densmore-Parent

Dedicated to:

CAROLINE DELORETO

Camilla (her Mom) and dawn, with Caroline DeLoreto's 'dash'*

Caroline lived intentionally with focus and with purpose! She was a true 'friend' whose last words were "Jesus is my Savior!" She changed addresses to go to live with Jesus, 'The King of Kings' in His heavenly home – just one day before her June 11, 2024, birthday! Thank you, Caroline, for your passion and for leaving us your example of living well every day! <u>We MISS you so much down here, but we will see you soon!</u>

dawn

DAWN, FABIEN PARENT, CAROLINE DELORETO AND ADAM TAFT
* The "dash" – the time between being born and death

Cover Design by: Tamara Smith, UVM Print and Mail, VT

©Copyright 2024

ISBN

978-1-7342353-6-4

INTRODUCTION:

"Keep thy <u>HEART</u> with all diligence; for out of "it" are the issues of life" (Proverbs 4:23).

"Still" reveals how the Lord works challenges into 'blessings' for His glory and His honor from choices we make each day.

Jesus said the greatest commandment was: **"Thou shalt love the Lord thy God with all thine <u>heart</u> with all thine <u>soul,</u> and with all thine <u>might</u> and the second is like unto it, thou shall <u>love thy neighbor</u> as thyself"**(Matthew 22:37-40).

Jesus emphasized the importance of this in Matthew 7:14: **"Because <u>strait</u> is the gate and <u>narrow</u> is the way that leaded unto life and <u>few</u> there be that find it."**

One day, as I thought about these verses, suddenly I saw a 'vertical light" followed by a 'horizontal light' crossing the 'vertical light' and there was a burst of light in the center where they crossed. I gasped as I realized that t is our 'relationship to God and to one another" that produces God's divine power! When we align vertically with our love for God and horizontally with our love for each other, we honor God.

Moment by moment we are vessels for His use, in both 'good' and 'bad" times.

My life changed when I asked Jesus to forgive me and come into my heart and my Life changed. It has not been easy, but the Lord is so faithful.

"Still" covers my experience of going to God for His help during my husband Fabien's very challenging health issues.

Dawn Densmore-Parent

Contents

Chapter 1 – Divine Providence	7
Chapter 2 – Our Extra-Ordinary Life	22
Chapter 3 – We are His Hands, Eyes, Feet	29
Chapter 4 – Home to Homestead	31
Chapter 5 – The Offering	35
Chapter 6 – Mr. Fix it	39
Chapter 7 – Retirement	43
Chapter 8 – Life Upended	47
Chapter 9– The Hidden Blessing	55
Chapter 10 – Life AGAIN Upended	59
Chapter 11 – A Very Long Day	65
Chapter 12 – The Miracle Day	71
Chapter 13 –Small Successes!	75
Chapter 14 – Yet Another Challenge	79
Chapter 15 -Life Lessons	85
Chapter 16 – Believe	89
Chapter 17 Life - Moment by Moment	100
Commentary	101
Epilogue	103

Chapter 1 – Divine Providence

***"Be Still and KNOW that I am God"* Psalm 46:10**

It would be the arrival of a series of unexpected events that would require us to exercise a new kind of 'trust' in God! These began with my husband, Fabien Parent, being unable to use his left leg, which was the beginning of a stroke. His stroke was followed by bladder cancer and then by a severe heart attack, each event simultaneously occurred; one right after another. The impact hit not only him, but me, our family members, and our many friends.

To actually be*' still'* in THAT VERY 'moment;' when 'action' is required demands an exercise of 'extreme faith' in what is NOT seen. I felt like I was in an airplane, with all four engines running, full of fuel, on a runway awaiting 'take off'. My mind roared with unanswerable questions, and there was nothing to 'do' but wait and pray.

But as prayer was made, I experienced a 'stillness' as if I were on that *'plane'* patiently waiting for news about the *'trip'*. I longed to move forward, to know, and for 'action' to happen. But *'medical'* brakes held us back from our take off in *flight* to our new destination. We "patiently waited' for all the physicians to address each issue. It would take 6 months before I would feel like we received long awaited words: "Cleared for take-off –go to runway '5': "HOME". The "non-active time' required the exercise of 'stillness' in a deep abiding faith in God, just waiting in an 'on' position. Here, the importance of prayer, and daily quiet time became very clear. Friends came and prayed for, and with us, which made all the difference. There was no way for us to 'know' how we would get through it all.

Each morning, my day began with time alone with God reading the words from the Bible. Then, I would pour out my heart to the Lord. I asked Him to take my fear and to help me to trust His promises in the Bible. Each day His Holy Spirit provided an ability for me to be 'still' and just listen for the leading of His Holy Spirit.

As I reviewed key Bible verses, I gained confidence that God **was** working these things together for His glory and for our good _in His time_. Each day, I would say to the Lord, 'Not my will but Thy will be done."

Both of us had plenty of _"time"_ to 'think' and to be grateful for the 'time' we had together. I thought about my life challenges, how we met, how we ended up married, as well as our incredible life together. My heart's desire was for us to **'_still"_** continue to enjoy each other! I had a **new** appreciation for _my "Fabien'_, as well as for **my** family, for **his** family, and for **our church** family, _my lifetime friends, and for everyone_ who showed up to help us in unexpected ways.

Fabien's life _and my life_ had come to an abrupt **HALT!** The 'medical system' was unfamiliar; Foreign to us. We had not ever required any extensive stays in emergency rooms, or within Intensive Care Units (ICU's). Now, we lived in 'it' -- day after day. It reminded me of the movie "**Terminal**" with Tom Hanks navigating living in an airport. I recalled a writing of Charles Spurgeon: "Offer the Lord **nothing** that has **NOT cost you something**." Our circumstances contained 'a great price'! So many people gave us their 'time' and 'help' and 'prayers' in our time of need. True sacrifices were made for 'us'. This produced an extreme desire to recognize individuals; especially nurses, physicians, and physician's assistants with a sincere 'thank you' for being there for us.

My small 'gift packs' (made for the London trip) were used as 'thank you' gifts.

The Unusual Timing

Fabien's hospital stays occurred over our 8th wedding anniversary, Fabien's Birthday, and during the 2023 holidays: Thanksgiving, Christmas and New Year's. There were many medical personnel who worked on these holidays to help us, and others in need. These individuals truly gave that kind of "sacrificial offering" to us and to God as well! I went out of my way to say 'thank you' to each person who helped us during our unusual medical time of need.

The Lord provided me with a song: "Be Thou My Vision" which played over and over in my mind. Originally written by Mary Elizabeth Byrne in Ireland as, "Bí Thusa 'mo Shúile".

Its English translation gripped me:

"Still be My Vision O Lord of My Heart."

Be Thou my Vision, O Lord of my heart.
Be all else but naught to me, save that Thou art.
My best thought by day or by night
Waking or sleeping, Thy presence my light.

Be Thou my WISDOM and be Thou my true WORD.
Thou ever with me, and I with Thee, Lord.
Thou my great Father, and I Thy true son,
Thou in me dwelling, and I with Thee one.

Be Thou my Breastplate, my Sword for the fight.
Thou my whole Armor, Thou my true Might.
Thou my soul's Shelter, Thou my Strong Tower.
O raise Thou me heavenward, great Power of my Power.

Riches I heed not, nor man's empty praise,
Thou mine inheritance, now and always;'
Thou and Thou only the first in my heart,
High King of heaven, my treasure Thou art.

Great Heart of my own heart, whatever befall,
STILL be Thou my Vision, O Ruler of all.
High King of heaven, Thou heaven's bright Sun,
Grant me its joys, after victory is won.
STILL be Thou my Vision, O Ruler of all.

These words conveyed to my heart my deep-seated need to rely upon God – the Creator of Heaven and earth. What was totally 'unexpected' had arrived when least expected.

We found ourselves embraced by people who would provide a 'net' of protection as well as a 'band' of security. Fabian and I had been on the 'giving end'; **NOW** we were on the *"receiving"* end – needing support and needing encouragement.

Looking Back

During my time spent in the hospital not knowing how things would turn out, I began to reflect and think about all the things in my life that had happened. My life had many twists and turns. Like a quilt, I could see that each event contained the hand of God moving and helping me to have 'faith" in the power of God. The incredible way in which my life had unfolded amazed me! Especially the way that Fabien had become my husband!

Fabien and I were both previously married and divorced. He for 32 years; me for 23 years. We both had been alone for a long time: he for 14 years; me for 18 years. We both had made 'efforts' to seek another partner; we both had NOT been successful: we both had lofty standards. Our meeting was miraculous, and my time waiting made me think of many other 'miracles' as well.

A "Life That Was Saved" Miracle

During my First Marriage there was one amazing miracle that occurred that enabled my then husband, James Densmore, Jr. to be at the 'right place at the right time." He had come home from work for lunch. Oddly enough, on that day, I too, had stopped for lunch at our home. As I went to leave after I had finished my lunch, we 'met' in our driveway. As I got into my car, he drove into our driveway in his car. We rolled down our windows and laughed. We had never "both" decided to have 'lunch' at home and met like that before! He was a Police Officer.

I left and went back to work, but after I left, as Jim got out of his vehicle, he heard an 'explosion' across the street at our neighbor's home and ran to it. Our neighbor's son was behind their home on 'fire'. Jim was able to radio 'rescue' as he rolled the boy on the ground to put the fire out. He then picked up the boy and carried him into his home and laid him down in the bathtub and he filled the tub with cold water. The Rescue team arrived to transport the boy to the UVM Medical Hospital. The boy was burned on 80% of his body; there was concern that he would not survive. Many prayers were made, and miraculously, after many skin grafts, the boy recovered. The reality was the perfect timing of the Lord had put Jim in our driveway. Had Jim NOT been home at the time, it is very unlikely the boy would have lived. The boy had been with two of his friends and they had built a fire. The boy had sprayed an aerosol can on the fire, and the flames had backed up into the spray can and the can had exploded in his hand onto his chest and legs. It would be years later when I was having my hair done, when I would share a Christian poem with someone next to me that would open a door for the event to surface again. The woman next to me in the salon was a former neighbor who recognized me and told me that my husband was a 'hero' for rescuing the boy that day. I was able to explain to her the Divine chain of events of us both meeting in our driveway that day just before the event happened, and how our short conversation had delayed Jim from getting inside our home and remained outside to be able to gain 'time' to help to save the boy's life. Also, how fortunate I was to have left before everything occurred that day. The boy would go on to make a career in law enforcement with a goal of helping others in the same way. Jim was never formally recognized for this 'heroic' action, but we are assured that a record has been kept in heaven and one day each of us will be recognized for our own extra-ordinary 'sacrifices' made, some of which will be known to only 'ourselves' and the Lord! It truly is so important that we recognize that this material world in which we 'live' is merely the scaffolding for eternity.

My Life's Unexpected Challenge
It was my close friend, Patti Pratt's death in 1989 that would lead me to counseling. Her death would cause 'buried' memories of being molested to surface. When I was eleven years old, we had new neighbors, and I was hired to babysit their two children and it would be there that I would be 'sexually molested.' My new awareness of this sexual

molestation impacted my marriage. My own inability to deal with my new reality would lead me to go and live with my sister. Jim and I never had children, and after 23 years together, we mutually decided to divorce. I continued to heal, and eventually did desire to be 'married" again, but my need to be in 'control' would prevent me from being able to move forward. During this same time, my father began to have problems going up the stairs to his home in Virginia. He knew I wanted a home, and an attempt was made for me to build on land that he had owned, but there were problems getting the land deeded back to him. A year later, my Dad suggested, I look at a home in Highgate Center and a year after that, I was able to purchase that home. The first two years I was able to rent the home out by the week for vacation renters which would provide the funds for me to upgrade the lower level for him to live independently. When my dad was ready to move, I flew down to Virginia to get him and we drove his car back to Vermont together. I would live upstairs, and mornings and evenings would include time to visit with him. As I enjoyed getting to know him better, I shared with him the many answered prayers that had occurred in my life. One night, he exclaimed, "Dawn, you should write a book!" His comment made me begin to write down each of the events that I was sharing with him, and that would lead to my first book with Ingrim Publishers entitled, "DIVINE ENCOUNTERS: The Reality of God Angels and Demons."

How Fabien and I Met

In 2010, a friend of mine suggested I check out the online website 'Christian Mingle". I was not really interested in 'dating' web sites,to meet someone, but to 'prove' her wrong, that Friday night I visited their website and did a search for 25 miles from my home. Amazingly, Fabien was on at the very same time, and 'winked' at my profile. We both had to join to 'chat'. We arranged to meet. We both immediately liked one another, but we were both looking for completely different things! He wanted someone to come and join him to live on his farm and I wanted someone to marry and live with me in my home, and to be willing to help me with my dad!

For five years, we occasionally talked on the phone, and sometimes, he would take me for a ride with him in his truck through the northern Vermont country roads that he knew so well. Throughout this time, the Lord would help me to recognize that I was safe with Fabien. Then I had a dream where God 'confirmed' that to me in an unusual way.

The Dream

Fabien and I went to church together. As we left the service, we went down some very 'steep" steps, Fabien was by my side to help me, but the stairs were narrow, so he held my hand to help me be safe going down those stairs. I stopped to look at him, and when I did, out of the corner of my eye, I noticed a small little girl on the stairs behind us who was now 'stuck' on a 'step' behind us, unable to move. I left Fabien and went back up the stairs to help the little girl to get down the stairs. As I approached her, I saw Fabien turn around and come back up the stairs as well to help me and her. As I took her hand, I leaned down and said, "You are safe now, we are here to help you!" As I looked into her face, I suddenly realized the little girl was 'me" at a young age'! I began to tell Fabien, but suddenly I woke up! It had been a DREAM! My heart rejoiced! The Lord gifted me a 'dream' and I was no longer afraid of being close to him! But now he was afraid of getting married, for fear of being abandoned again.

God's Amazing Ways

In 2015 during one of our get togethers, Fabien said, "What would you say if I asked you to marry me?" His question made me laugh. I touched his forehead and asked, "Are you sick?" But 'no' he was serious. On September 19, 2015, we had a small wedding on his farm in Sheldon, Vermont. My sister officiated as a licensed minister. My Dad made our wedding but would take his trip to heaven on December 1, 2015.

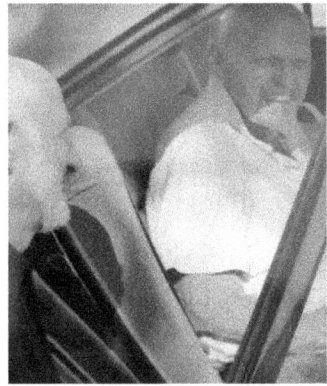 

Fabien and my dad – Our Wedding picture

The night my dad passed, I awoke hearing his voice, "I am coming down to talk with you!" I immediately woke Fabien up and told him, "My dad just talked to me from the other side!" That morning during my devotional time, my reading from the Bible was about 'measurements'. My dad had been a farmer and a carpenter, and Ephesians 3:17-19 was my reading:

"That Christ may dwell in your hearts by faith; that ye, being rooted and grounded in love, May be able to comprehend with all saints what is the breadth, and length, and depth, and height; And to know the love of Christ, which passeth knowledge, that ye might be filled with all the fulness of God."

My Charles Spurgeon reading also was powerful: "Pay no attention to one half asleep'. My dad had let me know he now understood the importance of placing God first in all that we say and do!

A Discovery - Eight years later-

It would be during a random conversation with Fabien, that we would realize that we had gone to the same school, together. He was a first-year student at St. Mary's High School, and I was in the same building in 8th grade. This was a 'catholic school' and due to an incident of a high school student getting together with an underclassman, the nuns had made an invisible barrier in the hallway that we were told not to 'cross'. High school students had one entrance where they came in and went up the stairs to their classes, and 7th and 8th grade students entered from a side door to get to their classrooms. After class, I would stand in our hallway and watch the upper-class young men going out. One day, I noticed a young man who wore 'white pants". He would come down the stairs and he would look my way. He had light blue eyes and blonde wavy hair. I began waiting for him and looking for him. One day he came down the stairs and turned and put his leg up against the wall. Then, he turned around and looked right at me. When I told Fabien about this encounter, he told me that he had a pair of 'white pants 'that he wore to school back then. His Mom would wash them every night so he could wear them again the next day. We both were quiet as we realized we had flirted with each other when he was in high school and when I was in was 8th grade. As we continued to talk, we realized that my best friend in high school had received written notes from Fabien. She had told me she was going to marry this man that had written her the notes! I was truly awed that she felt like that, but she had made me remember my blonde-haired, blue-eyed man, and I wondered, "What ever happened to him!?" I never saw him after that year. They moved the high school to a different location. Fabien would marry another, Debbie, and not my friend, and he and I never did see one another again after that year. The next morning, I got out 'old pictures' from 1968. As we looked at the pictures, we knew Fabien was indeed the handsome guy that I flirted with in 8th grade.

Fabien and I were also quite surprised to learn that Fabien went to school with my cousin Nancy Codding Greene, very well known for her sunny disposition.

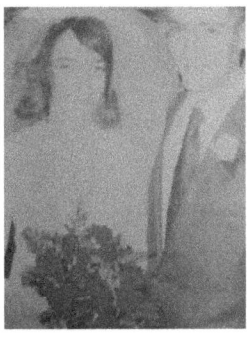

Debbie and Fabien

Fabien

Fabien married Debbie, his high school sweetheart and they had 4 beautiful children: 3 boys and 1 girl. Even though they divorced in 2000, Fabien and Debbie remain friends. Their 4 children married to produce 7 grandchildren and 4 great grandchildren with another one on the way!

Fabien's family gathering - November 2023

Life Interrupted

As Fabien and I travelled to celebrate our 8th wedding anniversary on September 19, 2023, he started driving down the middle of the road. That was the beginning of a 'stroke' that would take us to the Emergency Room with doctors attempting to determine what was wrong.

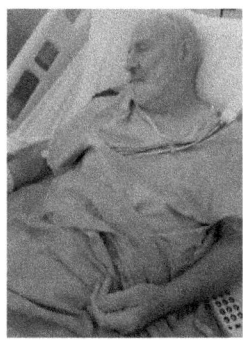
Fabien in hospital

The Incredible Team of Doctors

Neither Fabien nor I had been hospitalized, making the experience quite daunting for both of us. We were blessed by our first encounter with "D" who became a true solace in the midst of our 'storm'. Fabien continued to decline. He lost use of his left arm and left hand, as well as his left leg. He experienced some swallowing issues, as well as trouble with his speech. "D" was a part of a 'team of physicians' that visited us after we were assigned to a room at the University of Vermont (UVM) Medical Center Hospital. It would take time to process the many scans and X-rays, but a determination was made that 'plaque' from an artery in his neck on the right side, had travelled to his brain, and short circuited the signaling process to the left side of his body. Many cords and wires were added to Fabien's chest to monitor his heart and a catheter was added as well.

"D" was a 'lifeline' of 'hope'. He explained that Fabien was eligible and had been approved to be transferred to the UVM Fanny Allen Rehabilitation Center in Colchester, Vermont. Fabien, although 73, was in great physical condition and had not lost his strength within his right arm, hand and leg and foot. "D" assured us that Fabien would be able to recover. We would learn that there were only 20 beds available at this rehab center but also that it was one of the best places for recovery. Prayers were made that a room would become available for Fabien. Surprisingly, the next day a room did open up and Fabien was transported via ambulance to the facility to begin his rehab program.

Our Incredible Families

At the time of the stroke, Fabien was putting up wood in our woodshed.
Our routines for Fall and the Winter season had just begun.
Fabien's family and my family came to help! This was such a relief!
Their help allowed us to focus on the path ahead of us.
We learned how to lean into their doing 'things" for us.

Priceless Church Support

We also gained a new appreciation for the value of our being members of a church, who knew us and cared about us. Pastor Dan Frost and his wife Brianna from Northside Baptist Church in St. Albans, Vermont, were the first to visit and pray with and for us. Many others prayed for Fabien's recovery. In the end many churches in and outside of Vermont prayed.

Our faith was being tested. We worked to not 'judge' anything before the time. We truly did not know what would happen! What we did know was we were there for each other, no matter how things turned out, and our friends and family were there for us as well. The key promise I relied upon was Isaiah 40:30 "They that wait upon the Lord shall renew their strength, they shall mount up with wings as eagles, they shall run and not be weary, they shall walk and not faint."

My readings from Charles Spurgeon also provided great comfort:

"We are as 'roses' cast off and cast into **the Still**. We cannot enjoy the process while we undergo it, but the results are such that we are ready to fall in love with 'suffering". Time is 'short', and it behooves each one to be working for His Lord that when he is called home, we may leave behind something for the generation following. **Happier still** we may hope to hear Him say "well done." "Flowers" by Charles Spurgeon

Bible verses also assured us that God knows all things!
"But He (Jesus) knew their thoughts" (Luke 6:8).

Chapter 2 – Our Extra-Ordinary Life

Dawn and Fabien 9/19/15 and 11/18/23

Our Amazing 8 years

After we married on September 19, 2015, Fabien moved into my home in Highgate Center, Vermont. His background as a 'farmer' enabled him to accomplish about anything that needed to be done! I became his right-hand assistant! I also came from growing up on a farm, and I was there to help any way I could! His keen sense of humor made the work 'fun' and full of unexpected laughter! From the day he arrived, he saw projects that he wanted to get done!

Arnold the Pig

One of our very first adventures began when one of my sister's called to ask if we were interested in donating 2 pigs to the 'petting zoo' at the local resort in town. We had already discussed having pigs. Now, we had a great opportunity to have pigs and not have to feed them all summer!

Fabien found piglets for sale at a farm in New York State. When we arrived, 3 piglets were available, and one was the 'runt' of the litter, very cute and very small. Fabien and I decided 3 would be better than 2 for the petting zoo, so we got all 3. We transported them in dog cages.

They were easy to pick up by their hind legs. We kept them at our home just one night and transported them the next day to the resort to their pen that had been made for them. We went every week to check up on them, and they were growing fast! Fabien would get into the pen and scratch their backs and each of the pigs would circle around his feet.

Before the summer was over, the 3 pigs were too big for their pen, and we were called to get one of them. Fabien prepared his truck so we could go and to get the pig. Fabien placed a 'calf pen' in the back of his truck with a wooden board to cover the front entrance once we had the pig. Then he prepared a place to put the pig at our home. He constructed a pig pen out of wooden pellet frames on our back lawn, complete with a 'gate' for us to enter to feed and water our new 'pet' pig. He was named 'Arnold" by our respite person who spends a weekend with us in our home every month. Now the question was just how to 'get the pig into his truck. He made a ramp for the back of the truck for the pig. Fabien was quite sure we would be able to just pick up the pig together, one on each end of the pig and just carry him up the ramp into the calf hutch. Things did not go as planned. The pig did not like being picked up! I had been instructed to pick up the rear end when Fabien told me to, so I did pick up the rear end of the pig, but when the pig began to shake its head, Fabien's head was pushed into the gate. He told me, 'Put him down!" Fabien got a blackened eye from it, and the pig peed on my hand, but we were able to laugh about it! Fabien then moved the gates inside the petting zoo around and that allowed our new pet pig to 'walk right up the ramp into the back of his truck, right into the calf pen. I told Fabien most of his ideas were great, but to pick up a 'pig' was an unbelievably bad idea. I would be able to use this experience with Fabien during his rehabilitation time, when he told me one day, "Just get me a motorized wheelchair and take me home!" I replied, "Do you remember you telling me to pick up a pig? -Fabien, you have some great ideas, but leaving and getting an electric wheelchair is just as bad as you telling me to 'just pick up the pig!" I refuse to allow you to leave, and you cannot go home without me! The Physician has a rehab program for you, and we are not leaving until he says we can!" Our 'Arnold the pig" remembrance was sufficient to get Fabien to stay and work to do the program!

We eventually picked up the other 2 pigs. All 3 would have to be 'rendered' which is a kind word for 'butchered' into bacon and ham.

FYI: It is not easy to 'kill' an animal you have bonded with. The reality of our world is that our own life requires the 'death' of life for us to 'live'. The 'good news' is there is coming a day, when all things will be made 'new', and the lion will lay down with the lamb and the Lord Jesus Christ will rule and reign into eternity in a perfected world that is to come.

The Maple Trees

When Fabien arrived, he had walked the property and was able to identify 40 maple trees   It wasn't very long before he decided to tap them so we could make maple syrup on location. He would set up his own maple sugar right on location. He searched and was able to purchase a prefab barrel that had a boiling tray which he would expand by adding 4 boiling trays and another barrel to accommodate the vast among to sap that was being collected. It was labor intense work. He would go out and gather the sap, and then he would 'babysit' the sap as it would boil down to become perfect maple syrup.

Fabien and his sugar rig and the hidden secret

The Hidden Secret

There was a 'secret' in the woods next to the sugar rig. Fabien kept an eye on it. Our neighbor's turkey hen made a nest right on the hill above the sugar rig. Fabien's responsibility also included making sure the hen was NOT discovered by visitors who came to see his rig. Fabien would occasionally adjust the twigs for the turkey hen as the nest was on a steep hill and her weight kept pushing her nest down over the hill. The hen never laid any eggs, but it was truly wonderful to enjoy watching nature.

We ended up making 6 gallons of maple syrup. He poured the maple syrup into glass canning jars. Because we did not use a professional 'filter system', we ended up with what is called 'sugar sand' in the bottom of jars, but the syrup was rated 1 to 4- fancy to dark.

Unexpected Answered Prayers

My commitment to help when and where I could for those who needed help, caused me to ask Fabien if he would be able to 'mow' my friend's lawn for a summer. My friend's husband had surgery and was hospitalized, and their lawn would need to be mowed.

That summer, Fabien and I went each week and did the lawn care for the family. I did the trimming, and Fabien would mow with his zero-turn mower. We joked that I always finished sooner than he did, and that gave me extra time to visit with my friend. It was during our last weekend of the year mowing, that Fabien noticed there were several piles of dirt that had been dumped in a muddy road. He said, "I see some 'pavers' that will be buried in that logging road." Once we got home, we sat and visited. I asked Fabien, "What are you thinking about?" He replied, "Those pavers!" I called and asked my friend if we could come to get some of those pavers. We were told that we could, so off we went with his truck and trailer. Once we had the pavers at our home, I asked Fabien, "What do you plan to do with them?" He told me, "We can create a 'patio' for a new 'firepit' area!"

When I purchased the property there was a simple cement block 'fire pit' with a wire grill for a top. Fabien was not impressed with it. Fabien told me he would remove it and 'make' a new fire pit in a better location for our fires, hot dogs and smores.

One Lovely Chicken

One Valentine's Day I prayed for something 'extra' special for Fabien that he would truly enjoy. I knew he loved deviled eggs, so I decided to make him those for dinner. When I went to cut the eggs open, I was surprised to see an almost perfect 'heart' inside one of the eggs.

I 'saved' that egg and placed it on his plate and told him, "I have something extra 'special' for you to show you how much you are Loved!" He replied, "Well that must have been a lovely chicken to lay such a lovely egg!" I replied, "Indeed it was!" We both laughed at the sight! The account of the 'chicken with a heart egg" is featured in my 2nd book "Experiencing God's Amazing Ways".

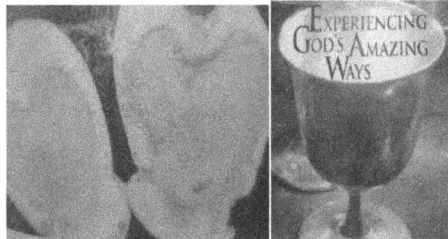

Fabien's continued creativity and unusual answered prayers would lead me to write three more books: "Experiencing God's Priceless, Priceless Promises"; "The Truth Shall Set You Free: THE PRISON LETTERS"; and "For Such a Time as This?"

A Divine Confirmation

When COVID concerns were lifted in 2023, I felt compelled to drop off my latest books to our neighbor friends. When I returned from my visit with them, I felt compelled to re-read "For Such a Time as This?" in case they had any questions. As I sat on our couch and read that book, I came to the chapter about the rapture. As I was reading that very chapter, Fabien came to the back deck door of our home and said,

"Come, you need to see this!" I put down the book and went outside with him. I imagined he wanted to show me some animal hole or an animal that he found. He brought me to the edge of the lake and told me to look up. As I looked up, there was a 'full moon', and it was shining with its reflection in the water. I said, "Fabien, do you know what we are looking at?" He replied, "No." I said, "This is the image that is on the front cover of my book "For such a Time as This?" Fabien looked again up at the moon and its reflection in the water and exclaimed, "Yes, it is the cover of that book!" I replied, "Do you know what book I was reading on the couch?" He replied, "No." I said, "Fabien I was reading "For Such a Time as This?" Fabien replied, "No way!" I replied, "Yes, and I was in the very chapter on the Rapture when you came to get me!" This was the exact same scenario that occurred with my first husband and my experience with a full moon, that I had no interest in whatsoever, but which would become significant to me that very night of June 28, 1980, with a literal appearance of the face of Jesus in the moon that night to me, not just once, but twice! There is no one who knows the day or the hour of the Lord's return to gather people from earth which is known as the 'rapture' or catching away of all believers from every denomination – but we are to be ready for it. The lyrics from the song written by William Clark Martin (1864-1914) affirm this truth to us:

His glory broke upon me when I saw Him from afar, He's fairer than the lily, brighter than the morning star. He fills and satisfies my longing spirit o'er and o'er. Each day He grows **still sweeter** than He was the day before.

Chapter 3 – We are His Hands, Eyes, Feet

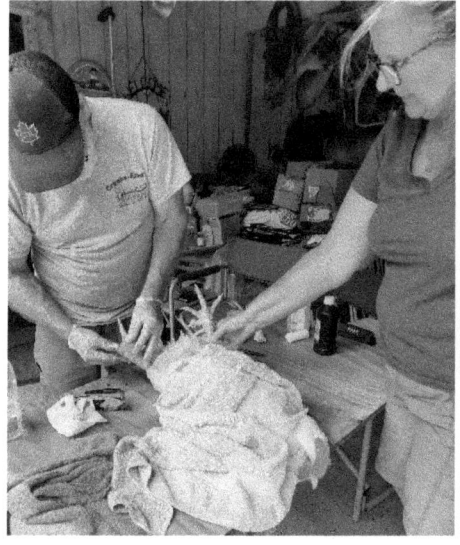

Fabien saving Sad Sam with Virginia Holiman, and Happy Sam with hen

Saving "Sad" Sam

Our back yard is 'home' to our neighbor's chickens and turkeys and to her rooster. Her rooster was given the name, 'Sad Sam". One day Fabien noticed that the rooster was standing mostly on its right leg. His left foot needed attention. Our neighbor agreed. A date was set for a 'procedure' to be done to help save Sad Sam.

Fabien cut a clear plastic bag and made a hole in one end for the head of the rooster and then he went and carefully picked up Sad Sam. He was not hard to catch, as he could hardly walk! I held the clear plastic bag as he placed Sad Sam 'head' down into the bag. Our neighbor came to help us with the work to be done. We expected a lot of resistance from Sad Sam, but he was totally quiet the entire time. Fabien was able to scrape off the scab that had formed on the bottom of his foot from 'bumble foot' and then put on anti-infection lotion and bandage the foot. Fabien had seen many procedures done by the Veterinarians that came to his farm. Week after week, the procedure of cleaning and wrapping and unwrapping the foot was done. Finally, the 'core' of the infection was able to be pulled out of the foot of Sad Sam. That day, I made a declaration that "Sad Sam" would now be, "Happy Sam" from that day forward.

Happy Sam had to stay in our calf hutch that whole summer. Fabien and I would go and feed and water him. We checked on him daily. It took the entire summer for him to be well. His bandage was changed every few days. One day, one of our neighbor's small hens came to the calf hutch door to join Happy Sam and stayed there all day. Fabien at the end of the day, picked up the small hen and placed her inside the hutch, so they could be together during the healing process.

The small hen would go and stand under the neck of Happy Sam. Each time Fabien visited them, Happy Sam would say, 'cock a doddle do". Eventually we let them both out on the lawn. At first, Happy Sam was hesitating to put weight on that left foot, but he fully recovered! He roamed our yard standing firm on both feet. He lived two more years due to the care and attention of our neighbor and Fabien. This is what we are told to do. To 'care' one for another and therefore fulfill the 'law' of Christ" and this certainly includes caring for the animals as well as nature!

We are assured, "God honors those who honor Him." We are assured in Psalm 23: "He maketh me to lie down in green pastures, he leadeth me **beside the STILL waters**, he restoreth my soul." This requires shepherds.

Chapter 4 – Home to Homestead

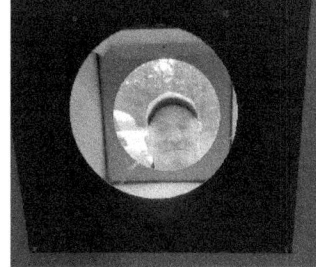

Perk

One of the benefits of Fabien is his ability to seize an 'opportunity' and then use his skills to be able to implement his vision. Although our home had multiple sources to heat it, we did not have a wood stove. Fabien told me how easy it would be to heat our home with a wood stove. One day he told me he had found a 'wood stove' that someone wanted removed from their home in a town close to where we live. He called, and we went off to see it. They were willing to sell it to us for an exceptionally low price and we took it. We had to go back with our friend to help load it and then unload it off Fabien's trailer, but now we had a 'wood stove.' The family also gifted us 'bricks' for its base.

Work began by removing our 'propane gas stove that I had added for my dad to make sure he was warm enough for a Vermont winter again, from his time down south! Fabien would then have to enlarge the wall hole for our new larger pipe. The removal was the easy part, the new soap stone wood stove was very heavy. We had to enlist help from my sister's son, Grant, to get the new wood stove in place inside our home.

A stove pipe outside to our roof also needed to be added. Prayers began because the stove pipe that came with the stove was not enough pipe to do the job to reach the roof on our home.

Amazingly Fabien found another internet 'post' from a gentleman who had purchased stove pipe for a stove but never used it. He sold the pipe for what he paid for it initially. The top section hookup would be the most difficult. Fabien and I discussed hiring someone to come and help us, but in the end, Fabien rented a 'lift', and was able to do the entire project all by himself. We initially thought we would use the wood stove only when it got below zero, but it did not take long for us to realize the savings were in being able to heat with wood all year long.

In the end we had 3 more sections of pipe than we needed. I brought the left-over sections to our local McCuin's hardware store, who graciously gave us credit for the unused stove pipe.

Redeemed

When Fabien arrived in 2015, we had two households that needed to be combined into one home. Some of his and my 'treasures' would have to be gifted to Habitat for Humanity. One of the items that Fabien had was a caricature drawing of himself riding on a tractor. The drawing came from an artist at one of our local fairs. This was something he was willing to part with, so he gifted the picture of himself to Habitat, and in the truck it went.

Three years later we would go to Habitat to look for an additional chair to accommodate our table which lacked 1 chair. As we looked for a chair, suddenly leaning up against a wall, we both saw the picture we had left there 3 years before of Fabien on his tractor! Fabien exclaimed, "Here I am, no one wanted me!" I replied, "Well Fabien we will have to 'buy' you back!" He picked up his picture and we headed to the register! He said, "I am NOT leaving myself here to be thrown away!"

One of his cousins was working there that day. As I paid for the items, I exclaimed to the cashier, "We just had to get this picture because it looks just like my husband!" She carefully looked at the drawing and then at Fabien who was standing close by and exclaimed, "Why it truly DOES look just like him!" I replied, "It looks just like him because it IS HIM! We brought this picture of him three years ago here, and no one bought it, so we are buying 'him' back"!

Fabien's cousin overheard the conversation and exclaimed, "Why

Fabien – no one wanted you!" Fabien laughed, "I guess not! And I am not leaving 'myself' here to jiust be thrown away!" When we got in his truck, I asked, "And where are you going to put this Fabien?" He replied, "It is going over my door in my garage!" And that is exactly where it is – our reminder of that fact that Jesus Christ 'paid the price for 'us' to also be able to be redeemed.

Chapter 5 – The Offering

In 2004, when I was able to purchase what would be our home, I literally went outside and got down on my knees and thanked the Lord for helping me to purchase it. I said a prayer of dedication for the land and everything on it for the Lord's use. I asked the Lord to help me to care of it, so that it could be a blessing to all who came to it.

Several of my friends were able to be with me in my home during some challenging times in their lives. One of the individuals who has been a blessing to us brought her 'doll' when she came to stay with us for a weekend. Fabien was gracious enough to assist with caring for her 'baby'. When I turned to see what he had agreed to do, I smiled and snapped a picture of him holding her doll 'baby'.

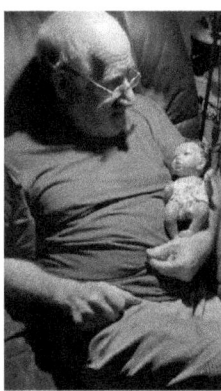

My own Pivotal Moment

My own childhood endeared me to 'dolls' and it was my taking my baby 'doll' for a walk in a stroller that would become a pivotal moment in my life. My family was part of a generational farm purchased by my Great Grandparents, Grant and Lucie Palmer. There were initially 6 girls, who would be followed by another girl, a boy and another girl. I spent a lot of time with my grandmother Merilda who lived with my grandfather Elmer on the first level of our farmhouse. I loved to dress up and I loved to play with my dolls. My other sisters were 'tom boys' and did not understand my passions. I truly was like a 'black sheep' wanting to dress in 'white' all the time on a farm. I loved using a doll stroller to push my baby doll around the driveway.

One day I decided to go around the corner of our house, even though I knew I was risking having my doll taken from me by my sisters. When I got around the corner, no one was there! But this action, resulted in me hearing an audible voice, that told me: "Play with your dolls, Dawn, you won't always be able to play with your dolls." Because there was no one around, I determined that it must have been God who spoke to me. I had been afraid of something that 'did not happen', and this truth continues to give me 'courage' to move forward even when I am afraid.

(

Fabien's Childhood

Fabien had considered becoming a 'priest' when he was young. His Mom and Dad would have him set up a communion table where he could practice being a priest. When Fabien got older, it was clear he wanted to become a 'farmer'!

Fabien's Hunting Adventures

As an adult, Fabien's love for the 'outdoors' and 'nature' resulted in many hunting adventures. His hunting expeditions include trips to Canada, Montana, Maine, Pennsylvania, New Hampshire, New York, as well as Vermont. One of his joys is to recount some of his adventures in the wild. Once when he was hunting, he and his hunting buddy were walking through the woods together. Suddenly they both saw 'deer antlers' poking above a fallen tree, where a big buck lay on the ground. When they reached the fallen tree trunk, they stood and talked about how odd that was to find a deer just lying there like that! Finally, his friend put his hands on the antlers to pull up the head of the deer. As he did this, Fabien saw one of the eyes of the deer 'move'. He shouted, "Put him down, he's alive!" His friend released his hand, but not soon enough! When the deer stood up onto its feet, the deer getting up knocked his friend to the ground. Indeed, the deer had been sleeping behind the fallen tree and was very much alive. They never did find the deer that Fabien 'hit' but when Fabien told his account, one of his friends said, "Well, that was quite a Hunt and Release Program!" Fabien's trophies include a black bear, a Cinnamon phase black bear, an Antelope, a Corsican Ram, a Caribou, an Elk, mule deer, Red and Grey Deer, many different pointed bucks, turkeys, a fox and a coyote.

Fabien 'feeding' his bears – and Fabien's Corsican Ram and Antelope

Chapter 6 – Mr. Fix it

Fabien's background as a farmer provided him with many situations where he had to be creative to fix equipment and solve problems. His unique ability to see 'possibilities' and to apply his skills is not limited to creating new things, but also to 'repurposing' the oddest of things.

The providential 'ways' of the Lord never cease to amaze! When a friend of mine found herself with an unexpected outcome, she ended up needing to move and then she needed a place to live. At that very same time, another one of my friends informed me of a home that was going to become available to rent. This would indeed provide the housing that my friend needed.

The Grill and New Patio Area

The home had a big back yard and when my friend asked for a grill, and outdoor furnishings, she received a donation for both! Fabien was enlisted to help repair the 'grill' that had taken a tumble and had a bent side shelf but was otherwise in great condition. Fabien used a block of wood screwed to the underside of the shelf and then took a hammer to 'bend' the metal back to its normal position. We also donated a patio table with an umbrella that we were not using to go with the grill.

Fabien with grill, setting up yard.

The Shed

Going for a walk with Fabien is no ordinary 'walk.' He truly has 'eyes' that 'see' things very differently! The importance of 'caring' for this world's things means you need 'space' under cover to store things. Fabien wanted a small shed.

He found one for sale for a fraction of the cost that was still in its box – it had been purchased and subsequently never opened. Once we picked it up, he unboxed it and set to work laying every piece of it out on the ground like an erector 'set.' Once the shed was all together and completed, it wasn't long before he realized that the front door entrance was allowing water to get inside the shed. He explained that he needed to add a 'roof' to the front of the shed. Within a week he was taking me down to show me what he had accomplished.

We had been 'gifted' a coat rack a few months before. Fabien had seen that he could remove the 'hardware hooks on a coat rack' and use the wooden base which a 2 x 2 board just the right length for the base for his new roof. He cut pieces of steel, salvaged from the replacement of our garage roof, and screwed them onto the board and then attached it to the front of the small shed! Presto! No more water issues within the shed entrance on its plywood floor base.

The added roof to the shed

The Bench

Fabien's abilities were enlisted yet again when a rocker bench of one of my friend's needed to be repaired. When we went to pick it up, Fabien examined the problem. This rocker bench break seemed almost impossible to fix. One side that held up the rocker base had 'rotted away." To repair this bench would require a whole added support to be added.

The beauty of the rocker was that it was made from twisted limbs of trees, which gave it a very 'rustic' look. Adding 'new' wood to make the repair would 'ruin' the authenticity of the entire artwork of the bench.

Nevertheless, we brought it to our home, and Fabien set out to hunt for the perfect piece of wood to match for its restoration. It took quite a bit of time to find just the right match of wood and then to remake the support for the slider rail. Once he had it repaired, we returned the bench back to its original location; to 'serve' once again as a place to sit and watch sunsets on Lake Champlain!

The Table

When Fabien needed a new 'door' for his garage, he found one for sale close by. When we went together to pick it up, he noticed a 'burn pile' behind the home that had a black box on top of the pile. Fabien told me, "I can't believe he is going to burn that black box; it does not look like anything is wrong with it!" I said, "You should ask him about it!" Fabien talked to the owner of the door and when he finished loading that door and paying for it, I could see him and the owner going to the burn pile. Fabien took the 'black box' off the top and looked it over. Soon he was loading that onto the back of the truck as well. When he got back into the truck, he said, "He gave it to me!" I asked, "What will you do with it?" Fabien replied, "I don't know, it is missing its top -that broke but it has the hardware for the top; maybe I can fix it!" The box was stored in our garage for two years. When our friends Caroline DeLoreto and Adam Taft purchased a home in Vermont, they needed furniture. We went to my home farm and they were able to identify several items for their new home. Then we invited them to look at what we had stored in our garage as well. That 'black box' was something they wanted to use as a 'coffee table' in their living room. Fabien began the work of making a new top for the 'black box'. He asked me to help him get the hardware onto the top that he had made for it, that would allow them to open and shut the top. Now, something that was going to be burned, had a new purpose! The 'box' became their coffee table, and that table was a big help to Caroline during her last days on earth, as it allowed her to set her feet upon it, which helped her to be able to rest!

Fabien on rocker bench!   **Caroline and Adam's coffee table**

Chapter 7 – Retirement

There was much excitement at the beginning of 2023 for both me and Fabien. I had retired from my role of oversight as Editorial Assistant for my last online scientific Journal. My position at UVM had provided me with an opportunity to work with Wiley and MaryAnn Liebert Publishers on four Journal publications for 30 years. Then each year, I would resign from one of them, until there was only one left. The end date for the last one was March 31, 2023. Finally, I would no longer be tied to the 'computer' doing online work from home. This opened a path for us to do more things together.

One of my passions has always been to be more involved with missionary work. When an opportunity opened for me to travel with Northside Baptist Church on a trip to support missionaries in Wales, I signed up to go on the trip!

The only problem was that the trip was scheduled for the week of our 8th wedding anniversary. The flight to London was planned for that very week. Fabien was most gracious, when he told me, "You have wanted to do a missions trip for a long time, Go!" With his approval, I attended the preparatory meetings with others who would go and made my payments to cover the costs for housing and the flight. The odd thing about the very first meeting for those that were going was, I actually heard a very small voice tell me, "You will not be going on this trip." My mind responded, "Yes, Fabien told me I can go, and I have signed up to go!" And I thought no more about it!

The Divine Interruption of 'My' Plan

But the closer the date came, the more my 'heart' felt uneasy. Finally, I yielded to the Lord, and sent an email to the Pastor explaining that there were some things that concerned me, and I was not comfortable being across the ocean, and suggested that he 'gift' my trip to someone else who might be able to go in my place.

One of the following weeks after church service, the Lord told me, 'Go to the Ladies Room". I did not have to use the facility, but the prompting to 'go' was extraordinarily strong, so at the end of the last song, I left the sanctuary and entered the lady's bathroom. There was a woman at the sink. We chatted, and she excitedly told me she was going to Wales, I shared with her that I had signed up but was not going to go. As we talked, I asked her what her name was, her middle name was my name. Then she told me she had something to tell me, and yes, she was the one that was getting to fill my slot. We hugged and I began to pray for the entire group and their efforts in this regard.

After the return from this trip, this woman came and 'gifted me' two hats, one from Wales, and one from London. She had no idea that had I been able to go on the trip, I would have purchased a hat from both locations.

As she gifted me the hats, she told me the trip had a profound impact on her. My heart rejoiced that she had gained a new perspective from the trip, and the Lord had 'honored me' with 'hats' from both places.

The Divine Timing of it All!

There was no way for me to have known that Fabien would experience a 'stroke' just as the trip was taking place.

Unexpected Blessings

When another friend learned of what had happened, she told me she had hats from London for me as well. In the end I was gifted a total of 5 hats – 2 more from London and another 1 to add to the 2 my new church friend bought for me:1 from London and 1 from Wales.

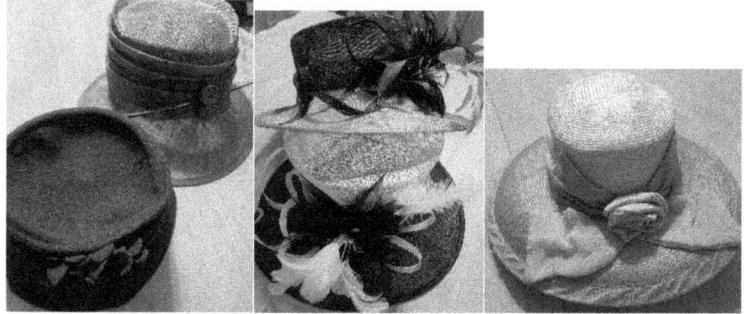

Wales & London hats   2 London Hats   Additional Hat

Still

Chapter 8 – Life Upended

The Trigger for the Stroke

The night before the stroke, Fabien had added a cover over our wood and had decided to go back out after dinner and finish tossing the wood up under that covered area. When he came back inside that night, he told me, "My neck is very sore." He was quite sure he had hurt it when he tossed all that wood.

Our Wedding Anniversary – September 19

The next day September 19th was our wedding anniversary, which would be followed on the 20th by Fabien's Birthday. One of his sons stopped to bring Fabien a birthday gift. Fabien went and put his boots on our porch. I watched as he stumbled with them after he put them on. I asked, "Are you okay there?" He replied, "Must be the boots!" They both walked outside to go see the wood pile. After his son left, we got in the truck to go to an anniversary dinner out. My plan was to take him to Canada for a meal, but it was too late in the day now to go there! Another restaurant we wanted to go to was closed when we got there, so we headed to St. Albans to go to another restaurant. Suddenly Fabien started driving down the middle of the road. He was able to correct the truck. He refused to let me drive but started driving slower. We decided to just go home, he just wanted to go to bed and refused to go to the hospital with me! At 11 pm he was not well.

I drove him to the St. Albans Hospital to be checked out. We were in the Emergency Room from midnight to 6 am. Fabien had limited drinking 'water' because he did not want to have to stop to 'pee". We informed the attending physician of this fact, and they gave Fabien an IV for dehydration and we were sent home at 6 am. Once we were home, Fabien went back to bed and slept until 2 pm

Fabien's Birthday September 20

Once Fabien got up, he told me he wanted to finish cleaning up around the wood pile. He went walking down with a shovel in one hand and a walking stick in the other to finish the job. I had taken an assignment for a few hours to do respite work in my home and told Fabien I was leaving to drop that person back home and would be back as soon as I could. But before I could return home, his son from the previous day called and told me that he and his wife were transporting Fabien to the University of Vermont Medical Hospital (UVM) emergency room. Doctors there did another scan from his head to his chest and found plaque from the right side of his neck that had travelled into his brain which had interrupted the ability of his brain to receive and send signals to the left side of his body. Fabien had had a stroke!

God's Providence at Work

I immediately called the Pastor and asked him to pray for Fabien. After he prayed, he said, "Aren't you glad you are not with us in London!"

Their flight had landed that morning in London, and the group would take a train to Wales. Indeed, the Lord had prevented me from being on the mission trip to Wales that would have placed me across the ocean for Fabien's life-threatening moment.

Fabien was assigned to a hospital room for further tests and procedures. I was told that if his roommate was okay with me being in the room, I could stay with Fabien. I went around the curtain and introduced myself that night, to our hospital roommate, "Andy" who was most accommodating and agreed I could stay. After I was permitted to remain with Fabien, a nurse brought in a 'recliner chair' for me to 'sleep' in. But it was hard to sleep at all in a chair. The third night I decided to just lay on the floor with a pillow. Once settled in on the floor adjacent to Fabien's bed, I finally went to sleep only to be awakened by something hitting my head! Fabien was tossing his pillows at me to wake me up! I got up to get him what he needed and went back to lay down on the floor, but a nurse came in at that moment and told me, "You cannot sleep on the floor here – that is not allowed!" The remainder of the nights were very 'sleepless' for both Fabien and me. The noise and 'in and out' medical activity in a double room was constant all night long. Fabien needed help to just stand up. Two hospital staff were present to move Fabien to transport him to the toilet. A special 'stand' was used to roll him standing to the toilet.

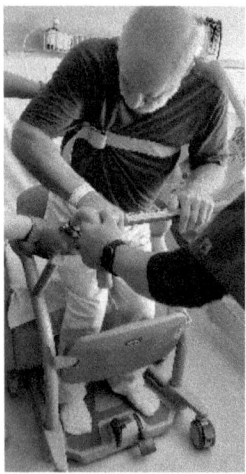

Fabien being moved with a seated rolling walker.

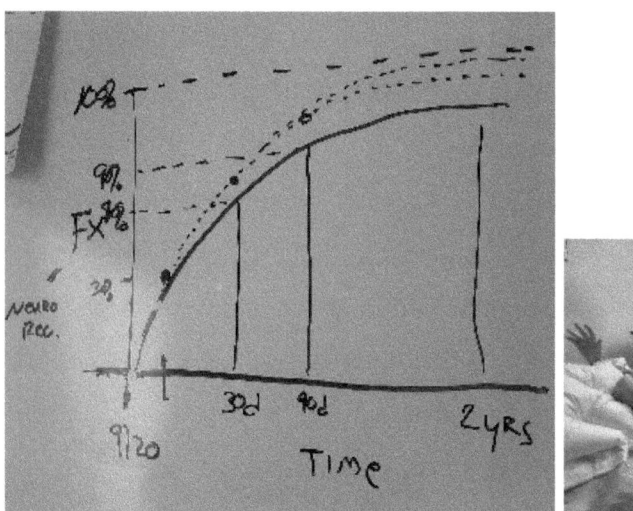
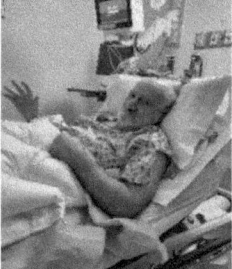

The Fanny Allen Rehabilitation Center Team

We were so happy when a room opened for the Rehab Center for him! Upon Fabien's arrival we were introduced to the Physician who used a white board to draw a 'visual diagram of a recovery 'timeline' of the progress that was anticipated for Fabien to regain use of his left side. It would not be easy, but it was 'possible' that within 30 days Fabien would be able to 'walk out'. This was almost unbelievable because Fabien could not even 'stand up' without a two-person assist upon arrival! Fabien quickly asked, "Can you draw anything else besides a 'diagram"? the Physician immediately drew on the board and said, "Yes, a horse!" Fabien looked at it and replied, "That looks like a sheep to me!" The Physician didn't skip a beat, "Well, drawing is not my level of expertise!" We all laughed! Fabien's keen sense of humor would be a delight to the medical staff who had their own entertaining responses. Having something to 'laugh' about was a real stress reliever for both of us, as well as for everyone who interacted with him! Each day there was a schedule for Fabien to follow that involved 30 to 45 minutes sessions for Physical Therapy (PT), Occupational Therapy (OT), and Speech Therapy (ST). The amazing staff were able to get Fabien to respond but he was getting exhausted. One morning, he exclaimed, "I just cannot do it today -- I need a day off!!" This caused PT and OC therapists to visit, as well as the Physician! These individuals worked seamlessly together like a perfectly tuned orchestra of hope and encouragement! They adjusted his activity time on that day, letting him rest, assessed his pain issues, and miraculously got him to change his mind and do the rest of the program for that day! And my cousin Nancy would 'visit' just when Fabien would be certain he could 'do' no more. Nancy knew what to say to him and he responded by doing the work.

Nancy Codding Green and Fabien

Fabien's Amazing Progress

From not being able to stand, Fabien was now standing and walking along the hallway on a rail, but he did not think he would ever be able to use his left hand or left arm again.

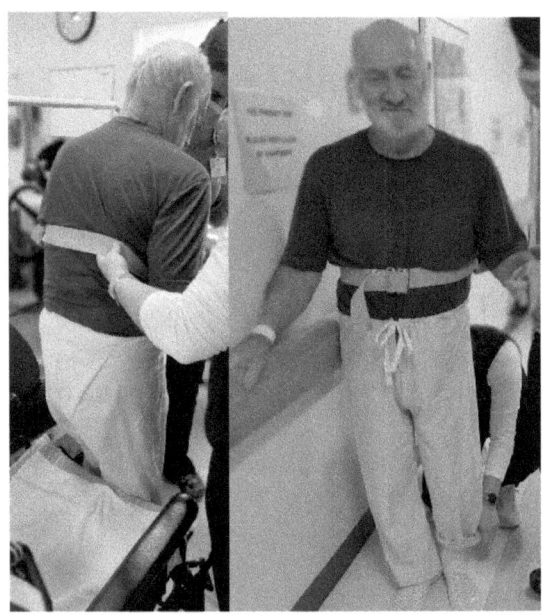

His designation for a 'two persons assist' was due to the risk of his falling. Each day for 2 weeks he worked; walking on a treadmill, and doing hand therapy, even tossing a rubber chicken to regain use of his left hand!

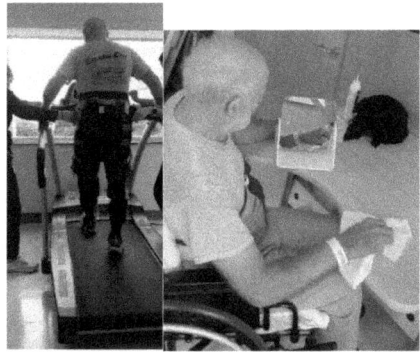

Within three days, he could see that he was indeed improving. What he wanted more than anything was to just be able to stop and go home and rest! He even requested an electric wheelchair! This was when I told him, "Remember Arnold the Pig!"

He was told that the program would work but he would need to do the program. I told him I was not equipped to manage his care at home, and that he needed to complete the program. I reminded him that the doctors in the rehab center were the experts – and they **KNEW** things that we did not know! Fabien finally agreed to stay and to work to do what they asked him to do. – just one day at a time!

I began fasting and praying that Fabien would be able to do the required therapy sessions. Each session was extremely hard for him to do.

The Odd Incentive

Fabien still wanted to go home. He asked the Physician, "Exactly what will it take for me to get out of here?" The physician instantly replied ny holding his hand up in the air and said, "When you can take your left hand and lift your middle finger up – like this - and give me one of these (as he held his own hand up with that 'finger' up); then I will release you and allow you to go home!" We were at the start of his second week.

I told Fabien, "Just do the program each day and give it the best you can and I believe the physician may let you go home this coming Friday night!" This became his incentive – just do the current therapy session and 'finish the job!"

Giving the Doc the "finger"

The following Friday, when Fabien finished his last therapy session, he saw his physician walking down the hallway towards him with his crew. Fabien shouted to him, "Hey, look I am able to give you one of these, now can I go home?" There was a lot of laughter amongst those around that physician, and at the end of that day, Fabian was released, and we went home! Truly the adage "there's no place like home" was true for us!

True Peace

'True peace' comes only from God and that 'peace' passes all of our own 'understanding'.

"We cannot know Thy **stillness** until it is broken. There is no music in the silence until we have heard the roar of battle. We cannot 'see' thy beauty until it is shaded. "   Leaves for Quiet Hours

Chapter 9– The Hidden Blessing

After Fabien's stroke, he started to have issues with his ability to void (pee). There was concern that he had developed a Urinary Tract Infection (UTI), so a urine test was done. The results of the urine test showed "microscopic blood" in his urine, and Fabien was referred to a urologist.

A date was set for a scan to be done of his bladder through the UVM Urology Department. The camera scan would reveal several masses within his bladder. Fabien was scheduled for 'out-patient bladder surgery' to have the masses removed. We were told they were likely 'cancer', and this could NOT be confirmed until after surgery through a biopsy. What was most amazing was that Fabien was not in any pain.

Home Rehab

Fabien was approved to receive 'home' rehabilitation that would continue his stroke recovery.

Continued Progress

During our first day home I suggested to Fabien, "Why don't you try to just get in and out of your truck?" He was not approved to 'drive', but he decided to try. Fabien was more concerned about getting 'out' of it than 'into' it, as it was his 'left leg that was 'wobbling'. Amazingly, he was able to get in and out, and he was able to drive the truck a short distance to the bottom of our road, and back to our garage! He knew that in 'time' he would eventually be able to 'drive' again! His success was truly encouraging.

Fabien also was able to get onto the Cub Cadet lawn mower, and onto his Tractor, which was easier to manage. The Physical Therapist arrived the very day that Fabien was driving his tractor in our yard. I was walking beside the tractor when we both saw his home therapist arrive. We talked about whether he would be in 'trouble' for driving it ,but the Therapist told him that she was glad he was able to manage to get on and off the tractor and approved him using it. The next day he added a bag to the back of the Cub Cadet mower. He then drove around cleaning up the leaves from the yard. He made several passes with the mower, driving over to me at our leaf pile, so I could empty the bag!

Fabien then took his 'chainsaw' and removed its 'chain' and 'blade' to lighten its weight and started to 'practice' just holding it without it being started. He would hold it in his right arm and use his left arm and hand to lift and move it around. His therapist was very impressed! He was creating his own 'rehab tools'. One Therapist told him he could use a 'hammer' to regain strength in his left arm and hand by holding it steady, and letting it fall to the left and to the right on top of his leg. This worked amazingly well and soon he was no longer having his issue with our firewood dropping out of his arm as he brought it into the house. Finally, we had just three more sessions to be completed for outpatient rehabilitation release. His date for outpatient surgery for his bladder surgery was finally upon us.

Bladder surgery

On December 21, 2023, the Physician performed the surgical procedure to remove the masses from his bladder. We were told that things went very well.

But Fabien did not feel well after the surgery and was kept in the hospital for two nights. Finally on Christmas Eve, he thought he was okay to go home and he was discharged!

Home for Christmas Eve!

When we arrived, two big presents were waiting for us -one for Fabien and one for me! Our respite person was scheduled for that weekend. Once he arrived, we enjoyed a small meal, and opened Christmas presents. Fabien was gifted an electric chainsaw by one of his sons; and they gifted me, -yes – a hat! Our respite person liked his gift of a Celtics sports jacket. We were very excited to be 'home"! All of us went to bed early!

Fabien home after bladder surgery with our respite person

We would be challenged to lean even harder into faith in what is not seen! We had no idea what was ahead of us that very night!

We both were so happy to be 'home'! We both were ready for any kind of 'new normal". We truly had no idea what we would be facing. There was no way for us to even have been able to prepare for any of it. Truly the only place for any kind of 'peace' for either of us would be in our having an ability to just surrender and go with the flow.

ABANDONED

Utterly abandoned! No will of my own.

For time and for eternity, His, and His alone.

All my plans and purposes lost in His sweet will,

Having nothing, yet in Him all things possessing **still.**

Lo! He comes and fills me, Holy spirit sweet!

I, in Him, and satisfied, in Him, complete! –

Author Unknown

Chapter 10 – Life AGAIN Upended

December 24, 2023 on Christmas Eve at 11 pm, (the very night we had returned home from his bladder surgery from the UVM Medical Hospital) Fabien sat up on the side of our bed and said, "I don't feel well!" I immediately got up and went to his side. I touched his head and found it soaking wet! I felt his hands and they both were freezing cold! He said, "Take me back to the hospital." I replied, "Fabien we need to call 911. I cannot drive and take care of you at the same time."

I immediately called 911. The local ambulance was quick to get to our home. Fabien was able to 'walk' outside and sit on the gurney.

Ice on the Roads

It was raining and the roads had a coating of ice. I was told, "Follow us with your car but be careful, the roads are bad!" I got in my car and attempted to keep up with the ambulance. Suddenly their speed increased so much that I was unable to drive that fast without endangering my own car on the slippery road. Soon the ambulance was going so fast that it was 'out of my sight'. I prayed out loud in my car, "Lord, please don't take my Fabien!"

The Heart Attack

When I arrived at our local hospital, Fabien was inside. I was told that Fabien had a heart attack in the ambulance. The EMT had given him a handful of aspirin which had literally saved his life. They now would transport Fabien to the UVM Medical Center. Again, I was told to follow the ambulance to the UVM hospital emergency room.

My calls

I knew our respite person was in my home with my sister but he needed someone to be assigned to be with him for the weekend. Rather than follow the ambulance, 'south' on I-89, I put on my flashers and stopped in between the on ramps for going north and south. I called UVM and asked for the emergency room. I told them my husband was headed their way, and that I would be there soon. They assured me they were aware he was coming and would take good care of him. I told them I would be there as soon as I could.

I then called my Pastor and told him what had happened. He prayed for us. It was early Sunday morning, and he told me he would come and visit us when he finished his church service. I thanked him for his support and for answering the phone in the middle of the night!

My next call was to Fabien's son that lived closest to us, and he and his wife agreed to go to the hospital to meet Fabien there. I then got on I-89 and headed north to go back home!

Alternate In Home Care and ICU

Once home, I called a friend, who agreed to come to my home for the rest of the weekend to stay with the respite person. I set things up for her for his care and packed a bag and headed to the UVM Medical Center in Burlington. When I arrived, I was escorted to be with Fabien and his son and wife, who were with him in the Intensive Care Unit (ICU). I also KNEW if I had done what Fabien asked me, 'Just take me to UVM Emergency with your car!", that Fabien would have had his heart attack while in our car. It was the ambulance EMT 'aspirin' that allowed his blood to thin, and kept him ALIVE!

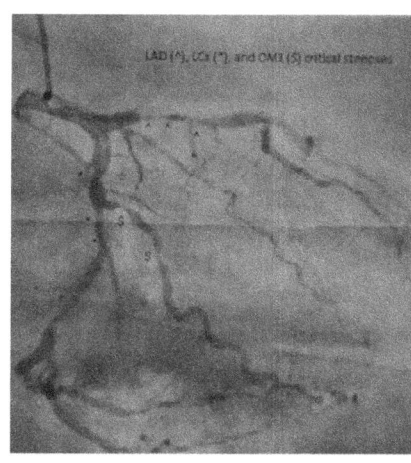 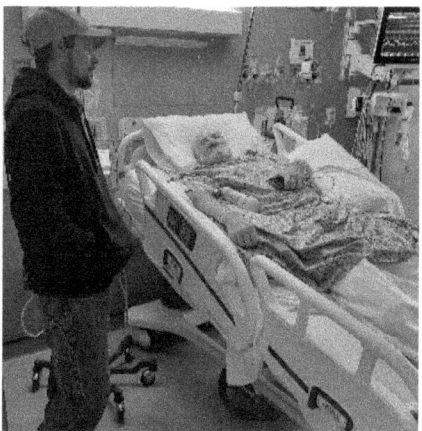

Heart scan blockages, Miller Room 3313 family visits Fabien before heart surgery

ICU

Fabien had a balloon pump added from his groin area at the top of his right leg to his 'heart' to stabilize him.

An ultra scan of his heart showed multiple blockages. We were told that the blockages were so bad, that stints could not be added. His blood was not able to get to his heart, and he would require triple bypass surgery.

It was December 24, 2023. The hospital worked to arrange an emergency surgery. We were told the medicine given to him in the ambulance needed to be out of his system for fear of him bleeding to death on the table.

Fabien could not 'move'; he could not sit up or get up to use the toilet. They put him on a catheter. There was nothing for us to do but to sit and watch the clock as it moved ever so slowly.

Our New Challenge

I truly did not want our situation to interfere with family celebrating Christmas. I decided to call just one of my sisters and ask her to pass along the news to the others as an appropriate time. Once again, I began to fast and pray, saying again to the Lord, "Please do not take 'my Fabien" from me!" I reminded the Lord of his answer to my prayer for a cat that would be "orange, female, spade, declawed, and Free". My heart and mind remembered that remarkable day when the Lord had answered that prayer and given me my cat "Buffy" who came with everything needed; her litter box, food, and toys. The Lord's answer to my prayer in 1997, represented the power of the Lord to do 'anything'.

Suddenly a 'vision' flashed before me of "Fabien in his hospital bed, being held in the arms of Jesus!" My heart rejoiced, knowing that the Lord was comforting me in this unusual way.

The Amazing Text

At that 'same' time, one of my sisters sent a text to me of a video of an 'orange cat' giving resuscitation to a grey cat! My heart rejoiced as I connected my prayer to the 'vision' the Lord had given me and this new video of 'life' being restored. For me, this was 'Fabien' and my own "buffy" (who was with the Lord): the Lord providing me assurance that Fabien would pull through. The odds of these two things occurring simultaneously, was assurance my prayer was hear by the Lord!

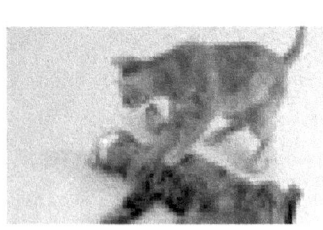 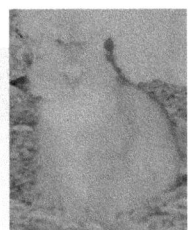 My Buffy Cat

The "Reality"

The day before the surgery, the heart surgeon came and stood at the bottom of his hospital bed and told us, "Fabien, you took a very BIG hit!

And there is uncertainty that you will survive this operation." They would do another test, but it looked like a good portion of his heart was no longer working, which meant that no matter how good the triple by-pass operation was, if Fabien did not have a heart that would be able to kick back in once the connections of the by-pass had been made, he would die on the operating table. This was 'chilling' news. But despite this information, I knew something else, that the Lord had heard my prayer, and my Fabien was going to pull through. When the doctor left, I shared with Fabien my vision of Jesus Holding him in his hospital bed and showed him the video of the orange cat resuscitating the grey cat. This comforted Fabien as well!

Intercessory Prayers

Pastor Dan and his wife Brianna arrived to visit and to pray with us. We held hands, as he prayed. We thanked him for coming and he assured us those in the church were praying for us. I wrote in my journal for that day my thoughts and some bible verses, as well as own prayer.

MY BIBLE VERSES:
"GRACE and MERCY and PEACE from GOD our Father and JESUS CHRIST our LORD" (1 Timothy 1:2).

"War a GOOD warfare" (1 Timothy 1:18).

"PRAY without WRATH (anger) and DOUBTING (unbelief)"
(1 Timothy 2:8).

God is a resourceful teacher, wise and strong, there is no need He cannot fulfill. He is a fortress when hearts are sick, and hearts are faint.

LORD, WE ARE WEAK WITHOUT YOUR PRESENCE. LORD, WE DO NOT HAVE NOR ARE WE EQUIPPED TO HANDLE THESE CHALLENGES. WE TURN OUR EYES TO YOU LORD! HELP US MOMENT BY MOMENT.

Even in times of bitterness, disappointment and suffering, God is FAITHFUL.

However rough and difficult the path REMEMBER that thou art being led by Him who has MERCY on thee.

My PRAYER:

Lord, Guide, and Lead: give us the victory over these trials that now seem to be unbearable. Make a way through the mountains for we do not see the 'path' from afar – we see only a tumble mass of rocks; show Thyself on our behalf and help us to WALK in FAITH and not by sight! Lord Jesus, I ask you to contend with him (Satan) that contended with us!

As we expected to have a way through, the physician's news said to us 'there is no 'way' to survive this. Fabien would die if they removed the balloon from his chest and that balloon could not remain there forever; and the operation itself could result in his death. So, either way he would pass. I felt like Moses, standing before the 'red sea' knowing it would take an act of God to help us.

"By the greatness of Thine arm they shall be as **still as a stone**. Til thy people pass over O Lord, till thy People pass over which thou hast purchased" (Exodus 15:15).

Chapter 11 – A Very Long Day

Prepped

December 26, 2023 was the day of the surgery. We had a very busy morning. His family came to visit –they were allowed in two by two.

Pastor Dan Frost and his wife came again to pray with Fabien. Fabien assured us that he had asked Jesus to forgive him and save him.

After the prayer, Fabien said, "Well I will see you after this surgery or I will see you on the other side!"

He had surrendered his life to the Lord's will - which was truly amazing to me! The reality of his frailness was right in front of me.

One of my new family friends from Northside visited us the night before with one of her sons and she also prayed with us together. At the end of her prayer, as we stood by Fabien's bedside, I confided to her that I could not imagine my life without my Fabien. Her eight-year-old son, standing beside her, looked up at me and said, "You cannot lose him, he will be with Jesus if he dies, so whether he dies or lives, you will still have him just in another place!" She and her son left as visiting hours ended, but her son's comment made me realize that I, too, needed to 'surrender' my own will to the Lord regarding Fabien's recovery from all these issues.

The Long Wait

It now was Tuesday, December 26, 2023. The operating room had just one surgery that day, and it was Fabien's triple by-pass surgery. After Fabien's family visited with him, they were told to go to the ICU waiting area. I would join them there. We all watched as the medical attendants pushed Fabien's gurney into surgery. We all shouted our best wishes to Fabien as he passed by the waiting area, but Fabien did not move his head or even 'wave'. He told me later that he heard the shouts but was pretty much out of it at that time and could not turn his head.

We were told that it would take up to 5 hours for the surgery to be completed. His family had been wise enough to bring snacks. Fortunately, the ICU waiting area provided a kitchen with a coffee maker.

The 'Word"
At about 5:30 pm the heart surgeon came to talk with us. We were informed that the surgery had been a tremendous success. Fabien had done very well and would be moved to the ICU recovery room. We were instructed to go home and get some sleep and that he could accept visitors the next day.
I was allowed to go in and speak to Fabien before I left the hospital for the night.
The relief that Fabien had 'made it' brought such joy.
One of his sons called his daughter to tell her, only to realize he could not say a 'word' he was so overwhelmed by it all. His daughter asked, "Did daddy die?" His son replied, "No, No! He is alive!" After he talked to her for a while he hung up and told us that he was surprised when he was unable to 'speak' – but truly relieved.
My own heart was filled with joy and praise to the Lord for answering my prayer and getting Fabien through the surgery just as I had seen in

the vision and with the text of the orange cat video that had been sent to me by one of my sisters.

But another battle was now brewing in the air.

ICU Rules

The first night that Fabien was in the ICU Recovery, I was allowed to go and see him and told to return in the morning. I called my best friend, and she allowed me to stay with her in her home that night. When I returned the next day, Fabien was awake but in a lot of pain. He would utter, "Ouch, ouch!" in a very low voice again and again.

All day, I would work to keep his mouth moist with a water sponge. My chair was as close to his bed as possible. The ICU is set up for the physicians and assistants to be able to quickly go from one bed to the other. There were no walls, only curtains, and the sounds of those in beds around us echoed in the air. This place was like a hive of 'busy bees' that moved from one person to another.

Fabien was able to drink and swallow. The air balloon was still connected to him through his groan into his heart area to ensure stability for his heart. That would remain inside of him until he had stabilized.

Even though I was his wife, I was considered a 'visitor' and visitors were not allowed to stay past visiting hours. I was told I would have to leave him again for the night. I assured him that I would be back for the opening of visiting hours in the morning.

I would stay again with my friend in town. As I reached my friend's home, my phone rang. It was the nurse on duty asking me to speak to Fabien. Fabien told me he wanted me to come back to stay with him.

I asked him to let me speak with the nurse again. I asked that I be allowed to come back but was told that he was okay and would be fine. I asked again to speak with Fabien. We talked and I assured him he was in good hands. He agreed that he would try to make it through the night.

ICU Hysteria

In the morning, I would be at the doors when they opened! I was in the parking area before then, and as I parked my car, my phone rang. It was Fabien and he was hysterical. He told me, "You need to get here right away, they are killing people in here and I may not be here when you get here!" I said, "Fabien I am right here outside the hospital on my way - just hold on!" As I entered the hospital, I called his son and told him he needed to come, that His Dad was 'not himself' and was delirious.

Fabien was not better when he saw me. He told me, "I heard a woman screaming last night and then there was nothing!" He was convinced she had died and that he would be next! He was sure they were coming to take him out as well! There was no changing his mind. He added, "I think I am 'dead' right now and that this is 'hell" and I will never get out of here!" His son arrived and assured Fabien that we were 'real' and that he was 'alive'.

Fabien seemed to calm down and finally agreed he was alive, but he insisted he be moved to a room. He asked, "Why are we in the 'basement' of the hospital? There are no windows, and I cannot tell when it is 'day' or when it is 'night' in this place!" Curtains all around me here! All I can see are 'dogs legs' walking outside these curtains!"

The Room Request

It was now 9 am, and I knew I had to be with him moving forward! Knowing I would not be allowed to spend the next 'night' with him, I asked the head nurse to work to get us into a room out of ICU. Enormous efforts had to be made to make that happen. He would have to be unhooked from the heart balloon and that required the physician's approval. Finally at noon, the balloon was removed, and Fabien was able to finally sit up in the bed.

We were told no rooms were available for him because he needed a Wing that had the equipment to care for him for his recovery. I called and asked for prayer from several people in different churches all over the State. Finally, at 3 pm, a room opened up and Fabien would be moved into that room. Fabien was still telling me that he would not be moved when in fact the 'crew' to do his move arrived. This room allowed me to be able to stay with him.

The incredible Team of Nurses

Fabien was assigned to the same Wing that we had been assigned to after his bladder surgery! The nurses we had before for that bladder surgery were quite surprised to see us again! I explained that when we got home that very night he had a heart attack.

Fabien's catheter had blood still coming out of him. We had been informed that there were some situations where after heart surgery, a total blood transfusion was required. We had agreed to that procedure if it was necessary; but when we, in fact, were told that Fabien would need to have a full blood transfusion, we were both very concerned.

The Elongated Blood Transfusion

As the blood transfusion procedure began, we were told that it would take 2 hours to complete. But new entry points were needed to do the transfusion, they were clogging, and those had to be changed 3 times. My prayers continued as the clock ticked. Finally, after over 3 hours, the bags of blood were empty, and the procedure was over!

Fabien had looked very weak and pale before it began, but after it was over, his skin returned to a normal color. He was able to sit up and was now hunger for food. He had finally turned a corner!

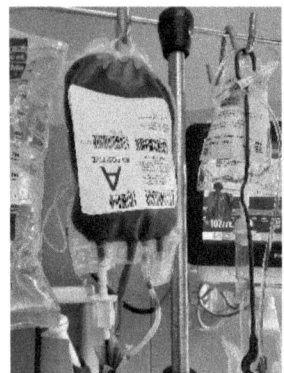 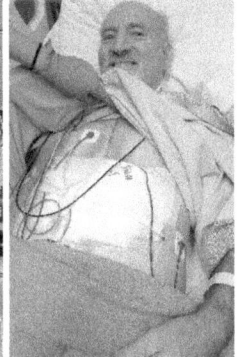

The Bible assures us prayer is heard in heaven, and an answer is on the way, long before we are can 'see' that answer!

"And they told him all the words of Joseph, which he had said unto them: and when he **saw** the wagons which Joseph had sent to carry him, the spirit of Jacob their father revived" (Genesis 45:27).

"Your wagons all the time, were on the way!
The Holy One Has set His name beside two men of saintly will
And calls Himself the "**God of Jacob**" still"

Fay Inhfawn

Chapter 12 – The Miracle Day

Faith Enough – to Go Home

The morning of New Year's Eve, we were told that *it might* be possible for us to be discharged that day. My excitement could not be contained. I packed my bags and put everything on a wheelchair and waited for his release. The 'ports' in his neck and arm needed to be removed from Fabien before we could go home. We were told we likely would be dismissed by Noon.

Noon came and went.

At 1 pm I asked a nurse if we would be discharged and was told no word had been given and that it was now getting too late for a discharge.

I prayed as hard as I could, "Lord, help us to be able to go home today!"

At 4 pm I asked again, "Can we go home?" The attending nurse told us she would check again. Amazingly she came back with a "Yes, but that will require us to be able to get you out in one hour, before 5 pm!"

The hospital pharmacy closed at 5 pm. I needed to get my things into my car, come back and get the script at the pharmacy, and then go and get Fabien from his room and wheel him out to the entrance.

This would be a 'marathon' endeavor that would require me to actually 'run with the wheelchair full of bags' to get to my car.

My car was parked a distance away. I immediately took that wheelchair with the bags of our belongings and headed out the door.

I went as fast as I could. I felt like I was running a 'relay' race. I got all of the bags into my car, and then drove my car up and around to the front of the hospital. I was told I could not leave my car in the front but had to park in the parking garage. I had no idea how to get to it!

I went back to the car and drove around and parked in a handicap area for which I had a tag. I literally had to 'run' back around to the front entrance and go and get the wheelchair that I had left at the top of the stet of stairs to return it to the front area.

When I entered with the wheelchair, I had returned so fast, that I was asked where I parked!" I replied, "I am not parked in the front of the hospital!" I continued down the hall to the entrance of the pharmacy to see our discharge nurse standing at the entrance waiting for me, it was 2 minutes to 5 pm. I took her place in line.

I was the last one to enter the hospital pharmacy – it was now 5 pm. As they handed me the script, the clerk walked me back to the entrance and locked the door. I had made it JUST in time!

I went with the script bag in hand back to Miller to get Fabien. The discharge nurse was just bringing Fabien in the wheelchair to the entrance as I went to open the door. We were indeed going home for New Year's Eve on December 31, 2023!

Homeward Bound

It was snowing, and our ride on the interstate was slow going home, but we were able to celebrate the end of 2023 in our home!

Fabien and I certainly experienced an emotional roller coaster ride, of 'lows' and 'highs' – not knowing how things would turn out.

The account of the storm on the sea with the Lord was asleep in the ship, with the Lord being able to calm those seas, was of great comfort.

"And he arose, and rebuked the wind, and said unto the sea, **Peace, be still**. And the wind ceased, and there was a great calm" (Mark 4:39).

Fabien slept for 2 weeks in his chair.

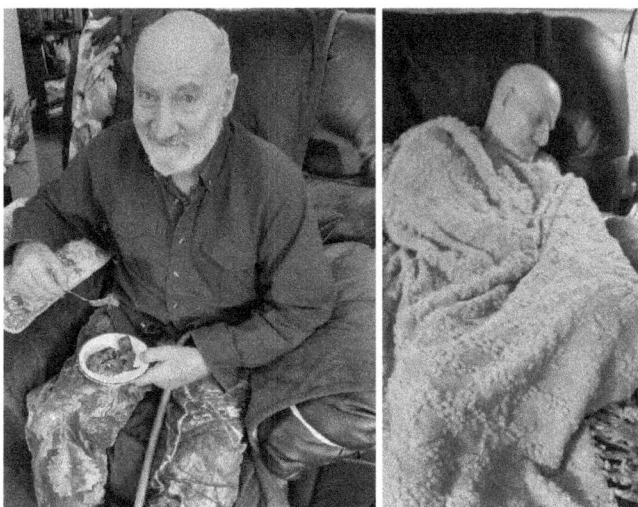

Fabien home with a cane and sleeping in his recliner chair ks after heart surgery.

The experience made me aware of the joy and the pain of the mother who had a son who was very ill, who ended up walking behind her son's coffin and was forced to **PAUSE! BE STILL** Selah, as Jesus walked up with some very 'good news'!

"And he (Jesus) came and touched the bier: and they that bare **him stood STILL.** And he said, *"Young man, I say unto the arise!"* And he that was dead sat up and began to speak. .and he delivered him to his mother" (Luke 7:15).

Still

Chapter 13 –Small Successes!

It would take almost 2 months of Physical therapy before we would begin to experience a new kind of normal in our lives. We were instructed to 'walk' at least 30 minutes every day. It would be on one of our walks that Fabien would discover a discarded lawn mower that had been tossed over the road guard rail.

It would be the very next day that he would get onto his tractor with a long chain to recover that lawn mower. The bank was steep, but he was able to hold onto trees once he was over the guard rail, and then with the chain hooked to the tractor bucket, he carefully inched his way down to that lawnmower. He hooked the chain under the carriage and then again used the chain to climb back up the hill like a 'monkey' to get back to his tractor. It would take several 'tractor pulls' and retightening of the chain to get the lawn mower back to the top of the hill, but Fabien was successful.

This one event would begin an entire 'chain of activities' that would begin to restore our lives to a new kind of normal.

April 2024 Snow Storm

When we had a large, unexpected foot of snow fall in April, he was back in his plow truck clearing out the driveways. His left arm and hand still 'weak' caused him to let go of the wheel while backing up to plow our neighbor and slightly rub up against the front of that mailbox. He stopped the truck immediately and looked at me and said, "Well that IS the first time I have ever 'hit' anything with my plow truck!" I told him, "Hey, I am so proud of you! you are plowing again – it is a new normal!"

Fabien rescuing a discarded mower, Fabien plowing with his plow truck.

The Unexpected "Cross"

During the bladder surgery, two tubes were inserted into Fabien's bladder that went up into his kidneys to ensure 'drainage'; would occur. These 2 tubes were scheduled to be removed. Fabien was told that each would need to be removed one at a time. that would mean that he would have to have the 'pain' from going up to get them 'twice'.

My prayer was that Fabien would be able to bear 'it'! When we arrived the Urologist went to perform the removal of the first tube. We watched on a screen and noticed a 'cross' of the tubes inside his bladder. The Urologist commented as well, and used his 'instrument' and grabbed the 'center' of the 'cross' and pulled; and as he pulled, we watched as 'both of the drainage tubes' were pulled out 'together'! He would NOT have to go up again after all! I told Fabien, "We have a lot of reasons to be grateful for the 'cross' and here is another one!" The attending nurse told us after the Physician left, that she had only seen this happen one other time in her entire long career! We knew the Lord had answered our prayers and we thanked and praised the Lord!

Enjoying Simple Pleasures

As Spring bloomed, we decided to swing by Caroline and Adam's home to check on their 'grass' to see if it needed to be mowed, to help them out. To our surprise we found a 'package' that had been delivered by 'mistake' to their home. The number of their house matched, but the street name was for the next street down. We were able to take the package and bring it to the correct location as well as meet some new people in the process who were out racking lawns. We then decided to celebrate by eating out! After we finished our meals, I used my sweet potato fries to make a 'happy face'! Fabien's French fries became a matching face as well. We looked at his 'food art' and mine, Fabien said, 'The red fries look just like you with your red hair!" "We both laughed. He added, "My happy face has way too much hair," and on that he ate his fries to create his 'bald' happy face head. His sense of humor was still intact!

Food Faces

Fabien loves BIG equipment, and he was able to enjoy getting to attend a "Logger's Fair" the very next day with my sister's husband!

"A merry heart doeth good like a medicine" (Proverbs 17:22).

Don't let the song go out of your Life,
　let it sing in your spirit **Still**.
　　　　　　"Springs in the Desert"

Chapter 14 – Yet Another Challenge

Once home, we were back to having Rehabilitation Therapists coming into our home to assist Fabien with regaining use of his body. This would be followed by being assigned again to Outpatient Rehabilitation to 'finish' the therapy for his left leg and left arm and hand. He worked hard to regain his balance. For 2 weeks we went 2 times a week.

Fabien lifting leg and balancing without holding onto rails.

His Follow-up Doctor's Visit

It would be on during Fabien's follow-up physician's visit that we would be told that during one of his scans they had noticed 'nodules' inside of his lungs. This would require a PET CT Scan to determine if these were cancerous.

The news startled both of us. There was a mix of happiness that they had 'found' these when they were small, but also apprehension with the news that they could be 'cancer'. The scan was scheduled. His Rehab continued, along with our combined efforts 'to not worry' about something that we did not 'know' anything about.

Life's Bootcamp

Our daily life felt more like a 'boot camp'. We were learning to live each day the best that we could as we gave our worries to the Lord!

My 'go to' verse became:
"Casting all your care upon Him for he careth for you" (1 Peter 5:7).

And we focused on the good news:
Fabien had use of his left side!
The events had drawn us both closer together!
His stroke had drawn Fabien's family back together -- COVID had created problems with us gathering at all!

The PET CT Lung Scan

The day of the PET CT scan arrived! Fabien did protocols of not eating 6 hours and drinking only enough water to get his pills down. We did not have to wait long before his main physician called to let us know that no cancer was found in his lungs.

The relief of hearing that news that day was so great that I was in bed by 5:30 pm – totally exhausted -from the 'relief' of it all!

We were living these verses:

"Abound in Hope" (Romans 15:13).
and,
"I have learned in whatsoever state I am therewith to be content. (Philippians 4:11).

The Follow-up Bladder Camera Scan

With the good news that the nodules in his lungs were NOT cancerous, we still needed to have the 6 month 'follow-up- camera scan of the inside of his bladder. The urologist physician had scheduled the camera scan to be 6 months after the initial removal of the masses that had been identified as cancerous from his bladder.

When a call came to move that camera scan up to April 19, we jumped at the chance to have the information from the scan sooner.

Holistic Therapy

The Urologist had recommended Fabien do 6 Tuberculosis flushes – one each week for 6 weeks -- to ensure that the masses would not be able to 'adhere to the inside of his bladder' again. These appointments were put in Fabien's calendar after the surgery.

After we got home, we investigated a variety of options as well as the 'efficacy' of these Tuberculosis treatments. A mutually decision was made to contact two alternative medicine physicians involved with providing treatments for bladder cancer: in Homeopathic and Naturopathic medicine fields. Appointments were made, and they gave us their recommendations.

Their recommended strategies that had evidence of being able to 'kill' the cancer cells, not simply prevent any cancer cells remaining in his body from being able to adhere again to the bladder walls. We started both therapies and followed them each day.

Benefits Over Risks

We knew that if we did do the Tuberculosis flushes in addition to the two homeopathic and Naturopathic protocols, we would not 'know' if these two therapies had 'worked'. The tuberculosis flushes were indeed preventing some cancers from returning, but we felt THAT therapy had no 'end' in sight.

The call was made to cancel the 6 tuberculosis treatments that had been scheduled by UVM Medical Center. The physician was not in favor of our decision. We re-evaluate. Fabien said, "If I do the treatments, I will have 6 weeks of them doing the 'procedure' that was going up his 'penis' with a scope each week, that will take 2-4 days each week to recovery from, and there is no guarantee that these won't have to repeated again and again!"

Fabien was already weakened by his stroke and from the heart attack. He could hardly manage getting through a single day, and adding these flushes would certainly interrupt his progress, as well as interfere with his overall well-being. Fabien dreaded even having to go back for the 6-month camera scan.

On the initial camera scan, we were told, "This will not hurt at all! Just wiggle your toes!" Fabien 'cried' during the procedure. He told me later he had never experienced so much pain in his enter life as a Farmer. Therefore the 6:1 ratio of no treatments and the reality that the strategy that we had decided to do, might work, made our decision a lot easier.

Our Past Success

Both of us had experienced Lyme disease, and we both had recovered using a naturopathic specialist who identified herbs and supplements to systematically, kill and remove the dead Lyme from our systems.

Precautions Taken

When the date arrived for the camera scan of his bladder, his physician agreed to allow Fabien to take Tylenol prior to the appointment.

We did have an alternate plan in place to move to Step 2 if the scan did reveal a return of the cancer to his bladder.

The Secret Weapon

My cousin Nancy agreed to come to the camera scan to be there for us. What a comfort it is to have 'friends' available who care for you!

The scan would reveal a very small cluster that the surgeon would schedule for removal in an outpatient surgery procedure.

Our homeopathic and naturopathic strategies would be updated to include the addition of 3 supplements.

The 2nd Bladder Surgery

The Physician would perform the 2nd bladder surgery to remove the small cluster that had been identified, which was very successful.

Fabien and I continue to focus on moving forward. The entire ordeal has made both of us much more appreciative of ordinary things!

*We cannot know thy **STILLNESS** until it is broken."*

"Leaves for Quiet Hours"

PSALM 23

The LORD is my Shepherd.

I shall not want.

He maketh me to

Lie down in green pastures:

He leadeth me beside the **STILL waters**,

He restoreth my soul:

He leadeth me in the paths of righteousness

For His name's sake. Yea, though I walk through the valley of the

shadow of death.

I will fear no evil: for Thou art with me;'

Thy rod and Thy staff they comfort me.

Thou preparest a table before me in the presence of mine enemies

Thou anointest my head with oil, My cup runneth over

Surely goodness & Mercy shall follow me.

All the days of my life;

And I will dwell in the house

of the LORD forever.

Perspective Makes the Difference

Most of my life I have thought of life as being a cup – half 'full' rather than 'half empty - being positive rather than negative. The Bible actually has an entirely different perspective and presents a cup that is running over with His blessings, even in the midst of the trials! This perspective brings great joy!

Chapter 15 - Life Lessons

Counting our Blessings

We are blessed that Fabien's mind and speech were only slightly impacted by his stroke, and that his triple bypass heart surgery did not cause him any loss of the strength he had regained with relearning how to use his left hand, arm, leg and foot.

The unpredictability of any day is something we rarely consider. Often it seems like 'time' is an endless commodity. This causes us to be blind to the reality that at any given 'moment' our entire life can change.

Fabien and I enjoy watching true life inspirational movies. During our recovery, we watched three movies that provided great 'take aways' were: **Regarding Henry**, **Buck**, and **Faith Like Potatoes**.

Regarding Henry

When we returned home, one of Fabien's lifetime friends stopped to visit. He was shocked to learn of the events that had occurred during our last 6 months. He told us, "Your situation is like the movie, "Regarding Henry" —when in a 'moment' Henry's life was changed forever.

The film features Harrison Ford as "Henry" and Annette Bening as his wife, dealing with the 'unexpected' event of Henry being 'shot' and waking up with a totally different life.

When Fabien and I watched the movie, we felt like we had lived this movie! We totally appreciated the effort required to simply walk, tie shoes, and remember words. Fabien's recovery mirrored Henry's struggles.

Events 'change' how we see ourselves and the world in which we live. They also impact our family, friends, and close relationships, for better or for worse.

In "Making Henry" the main therapist had been a football star who had both of his knees busted. When he was in physical therapy, he had to determine what to do with the rest of his life and had made a decision that being a 'physical therapist' would allow him to have a positive impact on others experiencing similar events. In the movie, the Therapist asks Henry, "Ask me, do I miss my knees?!" Then the therapist answers his own question, "No! Had I **NOT** lost the use of my knees, I would not be **sitting here** with you right now!" The therapist realized *that he had 'gained' more from his 'loss' than he had 'lost'*! His former life had been centered upon 'himself'; his new life was focused on assisting others to 'regain' their lives – even as he had done.

In the movie, Henry and his wife realized that Henry's successes had actually caused them to lose their close connection and appreciation for one another. His 'sudden life interruption' opened an avenue for recapturing the real meaning of life, which is not 'the stuff' of this world.

Faith Like Potatoes

The documentary movie "Faith Like Potatoes" features Angus Buchan's life. He chose to trust God and planted 'potatoes' which were never planted before in his farming area. His bumper crop of potatoes during a very dry season impacted the entire region. His message is to believe, pray and follow your heart each day!

Buck

The life of Buck Brannaman is featured in the movie "Buck". Buck had an abusive father. His emotional wounds gave him a connection with abused horses. Buck makes a connection with 'horses' and relays the reality that each of us can only connect with 'horses' and 'people' to the degree that we are 'honest' and able to accept ourselves as God accepts us. God's power is present to help us get through challenging times as we rely upon His Holy Spirit to provide us with correction without judgement.

GUIDE ME THOU GREAT JEHOVAH

"Hold me fast with Thy powerful hand
Feed me til I want no more
Be Thou **STILL** my strength and shield." William Williams 1717-1791

"Lead me in Thy truth and teach me for Thou art the God of my salvation, on Thee do I wait all the day" (Psalm 25:5).

Still

Chapter 16 – Believe

Fabien's recovery

It would be six months after the beginning of Fabien's 'trials' that Fabien and I would again be able to begin to help: when, and where we could.

When our friends Caroline and Adam purchased trees to plant for a wind break around their home, we were part of a team that was able to help them. Tracie from our Northside church volunteered to help, along with another of their friends, Scott, and a date was set to plant the trees. Fabien and I used our truck and trailer to deliver a load of bark mulch to their home. Although exhausted from a cancer treatmentCaroline and Lily, their Labradoodle joined us!

Caroline and Lily

A Farmer Solution

After the cedar shrubs were planted, Fabien insisted they be watered. My idea of watering involved carrying buckets of water to each tree, but Fabien had a 'farmer's solution'. He took his truck and showed me a huge barrel that he had created to hold 'sap'. The barrel had been part of his homemade sugaring operation and had not been used since we had tapped our maple trees and used it to hold 'tree sap' for his boiling pans. Fabien had modified a barrel by adding a water spot and air vent on the top.

Fabien and I put his barrel in the back of his truck bed and filled the barrel with water. Fabien attached a hose to the facet on that barrel and we headed over to water the shrubs. His plan worked great! He drove his truck as I walked behind the truck with the hose! We were able to water each scrub in record time!

Finish the Job

One of the lessons we had been told while in the UVM Fanny Allen Rehabilitation Hospital by his main Physical Therapist, was "The most important thing to remember is "FINISH THE JOB"! The shrubs would require continual watering of an area planted was over 2,000 feet in length!

Fabien told me he had a watering hose that one of his sons had given to him. After we finished watering, we got the watering hose and placed it along the base of the length of all of tree trunks. Adam got 'connectors' and hooked this hose up to become his new watering line. The watering line has 'holes' allowing each scrub to get watered. Adam had only to connect the hose to the spicket on the back of his home to their well, and then turn on the hose and run the water for just a short time each day.

Mulch to Hold Moisture

The next day, I returned to help Adam place black landscape fabric with shovels of bark mulch to hold the fabric down from being tossed by the wind! Adam then placed the watering hose under the fabric.

Still a Better Plan

Fabien came with his tractor and was able to use his tractor bucket to drive into the back of the trailer and scoop up shovels full of bark mulch. Then he would back out and bring the mulch to the 'rows' which allowed us to place mulch on top of the black landscape fabric in record time!

Soon it was evident that we needed another load of bark mulch. Fabien and I took the truck and trailer again and headed to get more mulch.

Another "Parting of the Sea"

As Fabien drove into the H&B Gardening Center on the day before Mother's Day, their parking lot was full of trucks and cars. I exclaimed, "Lord we will need another *parting of this 'sea'* to finish this job today!" It was 4 pm when Fabien turned his truck and trailer into their parking lot, and a 'path' opened up before us! Fabien never stopped, not even once, he was able to drive his truck and trailer right up to the area where the 'bark mulch' was being loaded by an attendant with a tractor. There was one truck customer that had finished being loaded who was leaving. I told Fabien, "Just back right up behind him!" Fabien stopped to let me out and I went and told the tractor driver, "We need 4 tractor buckets, please load it – I am headed inside to pay for it!" The attendant replied, "Okay!" I walked as fast as I could the distance to get to the Register inside the Gardening Center. As I approached the entrance, I saw a line of people waiting to pay for their flowers and shrubs. I told the Lord, "What now?! I CANNOT break 'into' this long line of people who have been waiting to get to the register!" But as I looked to see the end of that line, the owner of the Nursery walked in pulling a cart. I let her pass me and got in line behind her and got my wallet with the cash needed to pay for the 4 buckets. I tapped her on the shoulder and asked, "Can I give you the cash for the same load that we got the other day?" She said, "Yes!" She took my payment and asked, "Does "Brian" know to load it?" I replied, 'He is loading it now!" She replied, "Great!" Just like that! I walked out and back to our truck and trailer to witness Brian placing the last bucket full onto our trailer. I went and told Brian, "We will be the customer that paid in cash today!" As I got back into the front seat of our truck, I exclaimed to Fabien, "Well, God is also **still** able to part a sea of 'traffic' and of 'people'! We arrived with a prayer to the Lord, and we departed 'full' as though we had been the only ones shopping this day!"

The Promise

There is a heavenly realm that can only be accessed 'one' way -through PRAYER!

We gain access to the divine life, NOT through our own efforts to climb the mountain. This is what is called 'climbing up some other way'. Our link to God is through His son Jesus Christ who was sent on a rescue mission to earth. He lived a perfect life, and willingly allowed men to place him on a wooden cross. He 'died' a physical death. He hung between 2 thieves: one thief mocked him, but the other one recognized that something else was happening. That thief declared, "Dost not thou fear God, seeing thou art in the same condemnation? And we indeed justly; for we receive the due reward of our deeds, but this man hath done nothing amiss. And he said unto Jesus, "Lord, remember me when thou comest into thy kingdom. And Jesus said unto him, Verily I say unto thee, today shall thou be with me in paradise." (Luke 23:40-43).

Resurrected

Jesus was placed in a tomb, but God raised Him from the dead and for 40 days, Jesus appeared and disappeared. His final instructions were given in the book of Acts, as a cloud came and circled his feet. Jesus was lifted up into the air. His final words were, "But ye shall receive power, after that the Holy Ghost is come upon you and ye shall be witnesses unto me both in Jerusalem, and in all Judea, and in Samaria, and unto the uttermost part of the earth" (Acts 1:8).

"And when he had spoken these things while they beheld, he was taken up and a cloud received him out of their sight, and while they looked steadfastly toward heaven as he went up, behold, two men stood by them in white apparel: which also said, Ye men of Galilee, why stand ye gazing up into heaven? This same Jesus, which is taken up from you into heaven, shall so come in like manner as ye have seen him go into Heaven" (Acts 9-11).

There is a warning given by Jesus in John 10: "Verily, verily (surely surely) I say unto you, he that entereth not by the door into the sheepfold, but climbeth up some other way, the same is a thief and a robber. But he that entered in by the door is the shepherd of the sheep. To him the porter openeth, and the sheep hear his voice, and he calleth his own sheep by name, and leadest them out. And when he putteth forth his own sheep, he goeth before them, and the sheep follow him, for they know his voice. And a stranger will they not follow, but will flee from him, for they know not the voice of strangers."

Hear - Say

My own view of 'life' was originally based upon the many books on 'spirituality' I had read, and my own understanding, along with what I had heard other people tell me about the Bible. I had made my judgements based on what I *'heard'* and that is what I would *"say"*. When I shared these views about the Bible with someone who had studied the bible, I was told, "Seems you have a lot to say about a book you have never read!" That comment caused me to purchase a KJV Bible and read the New Testament for myself! My expectation that I could not understand the bible was NOT correct. I understood enough to realize that I had missed the entire point of 'life'. My goal had been to 'understand life' on a spiritual level so that I could gain control of my life's outcomes. After reading the New Testament, my desire changed. My goal was changed to a deep desire to be obedient to the Creator of it all, and to become a 'vessel' for His use and to be 'pleasing in His sight".

"The 'soul' should be our main care. **My soul stand thou STILL** and see the salvation of the Lord." Flowers Charles Spurgeon

"She hath done what she could" (john 14:8). Oswald Chambers: "I have not done what I could until I have done the same."

"Soon and very soon we are going to see the King" Andraé Crouch

Trust in What is Not Seen

I am aware that many may be like 'me'. When I first began to read the Bible, my HEART opened and caused me to cry out to Jesus to forgive me and remember me. When I asked to be forgiven for all the wrong decisions I had made, I cried, and received a 'peace' and 'joy' that has never left me– even during very trying times!

It is our 'heart' that matters!

"Trust in the Lord with all thine HEART and lean not unto thine own UNDERSTANDING, in all thy ways acknowledge Him and allow Him to direct thy path" (Proverbs 3:4-5).

"Delight thyself also in the Lord and he shall give thee the desires of thine HEART. Commit thy way unto the Lord, trust also in Him and He shall bring IT to pass" (Psalm 37:4-5).

"Rest in the Lord, and wait patiently for Him, fret not thyself "(Psalm 37;7).

The Bible reveals:

"Not that we are SUFFICIENT of OURSELVES to THINK anything as of ourselves, but our sufficiency is of God. For God who commended the light to shine out of darkness hath shined in our hearts to give the light of the knowledge of the glory of God in the face of Jesus Christ" (2 Corinthians 4:6).

"For we must all appear before the judgement seat of Christ that everyone may receive the things done in his body according to that which he hath done, whether it be good or bad" (2 Corinthians 5:10).

"Therefore if any man be in Christ he is a new creature (born again) old things are passed away, behold all things become NEW, and all things are of God who hath reconciled us to himself by Jesus Christ and hath given to us the ministry of reconciliation" ()2 Corinthians 5:17-18).

"To wit that God was in Christ reconciling the world unto Himself, not imputing their trespasses unto them (judgment) and that committed unto us His word of reconciliation (forgiveness)" (2 Corinthians 5:19).

"For He Hath made him (Jesus) to be sin for 'us' who knew no sin that we might be made the righteousness of God in Him" (2 Corinthians 5:21).

We are assured:

"All have sinned and fallen short of the glory of God."

There is NONE righteous, no not one" (Romans 3:10).

"For all have sinned and come short of the glory of God "(Romans 3:23).

"But God commendeth his love toward us, in that, while we were yet sinners, Christ died for us" ((Romans 5:8).

"For as by one man's disobedience many were made sinners, (Adam) so by the obedience of one (Jesús) shall many be made righteous" (Romans 5:19).

"For the wages of sin is death; but the GIFT OF GOD is ETERNAL LIFE through Jesus Christ our Lord" (Romans 6:23).

"For I bear them record that they have **a zeal** for God, but not according to knowledge, for they being ignorant of God's righteousness, and going about to establish their on righteousness, have not submitted themselves unto the righteousness of God. For Christ is the END of the law for righteousness to everyone that believeth" (Romans 10:3-4).

"But what saith it? The word is nigh thee, even in thy mouth, and in thy heart that is, the word of FAITH, which we preach: that if thou shalt confess with thy mouth the Lord Jesus and shalt believe in thine heart that God hath Raised him from the dead, thou shall be saved. For with the HEART man believeth unto righteousness, and with the mouth confession is made unto salvation" (Romans 10:9-10).

"For whosoever shall call upon the name of the Lord shall be SAVED" (Romans 10:13).

"So, then faith cometh by hearing, and hearing by the word of God" (Romans 10:17).

"For God so loved the world, that he gave his only begotten son, that WHOSOEVER believeth in him, should not perish but have everlasting life. For God sent not his son into the world to condemn the world; but that the world through him might be saved" (John 3:16-17).

"Let not your heart be troubled: ye believe in God, believe also in me. In my father's house are many mansions, if it were not so, I would have told you. I go to prepare a place for you. And if I go and prepare a place for you, I will come again, and receive you unto myself; that where I am, there ye may be also" (John 14:1-3).

"I am the way, the truth, and the life, no man cometh unto the father but by me" (John 14:6).

"A new commandment I give unto you, that ye love one another, as I have loved you, that ye also love one another. By this shall all men know that ye are my disciples, if ye have love one to another" (John 13:34-35).

"These things are written unto you that believe on the name of the son of God, that ye may **KNOW** that ye have eternal life, and that he may believe on the name of the son of God. And this is the confidence that we have in him, that, if we ask anything according to his will, he hearth us. And if we know that he hear us, whatsoever we ask, we know that we have the petitions that we desired of him" (1 John 5:13-15).

"For I testify unto every man that heareth the words of the prophecy of this book (the Bible), if any man shall ADD unto these things, God shall add unto him the plagues that are written in this book: And if any man shall TAKE AWAY from the words of the book of this prophecy; God shall take away his part out of the book of life, and out of the holy city and from the things which are written in this book. He that testifieth these things saith, Surely, I come quickly. Amen. Even so, come, Lord Jesus" (Revelation 22:18-20).

"WHOSOEVER shall call upon the name of the Lord shall be saved" (Romans 10:13).

That if thou shalt confess with thy mouth the Lord Jesus and believe in thine HEART that God hath raised him from the dead, thou shalt be SAVED. For with the heart man believeth unto righteousness, and with the mouth confession is made unto salvation" (Romans 10:9-10).

Jesus Christ and the Rapture

We are assured that the Lord Jesus Christ will return to the earth to establish His Kingdom where the lion will lay down with the lamb.

Between now and then, all believers in the work of Jesus Christ for their salvation, will be caught up off from this earth in what is known as the Rapture. I actually had a 'dream' of being pulled up into the air and being in the sky and then I woke up! It truly felt like more than a 'dream'. I felt myself lifted up out of a home through the roof, and into the air fully clothed and could see the sky full of people everywhere. My book **"For Such a Time as This?"** encourages us to be 'ready'!

John C. Lennox provides a glimpse of how things may unfold in his book, "2084 Artificial Intelligence (A.I.) and of the Future of Humanity". Computers do not have 'human hearts' It is 'God's love that enables us as 'humans' to truly be there and care one for another on this earth.

There are many who made it a practice to read the bible in themonring and set aside time to pray about the day. I have made this my habit as well. Once my heart is anchored with the Lord, the day takes on a new perspective. Harriot Beacher Stowe (1812-1896) rose at 4:30 am each morning to have silence before the rush of the day to experience **being still** with the Lord. Her song "Still, Still with Thee" speaks of gaining peace for each day:

Still, still with Thee, as to each newborn morning,
A fresh and **solemn splendor still** is given,
So does this blessed consciousness, awaking,
Breathe each day nearness unto Thee and Heaven.

Chapter 17   Life - Moment by Moment

"Beloved, let us love one another for love is of God, and everyone that loveth is of God and is known of God." (1 John 4:7)

Life's ultimate purpose is LOVE.

We need GOD's love, present, living within us to be able to OVERCOME this world's jungle of indifference, hatred, ingratitude, discouragement, disasters, and dismays.

For it is only from God's presence within us that we can:

LOVE where there is 'hate',

FORGIVE when we are 'offended',

ENCOURAGE those who are 'discouraged.'

And be a 'vessel' of the LOVE of God to others.

LOVE is the whole meaning of life:

"God is **LOVE**" (1 John 4:8).

We are assured that the Lord knows all things and we can be encouraged to know what Jesus said about following Him:

"If any man serve me, **him** will my father honor."

Jesus (John 12:26)

Commentary

"Still"

To be 'still' in our busy non-stop world, requires that we 'stop' and 'consider' God's promises written in the Bible. When we believe and act upon God's promises, we are empowered to realign our priorities and we become enabled by His Holy Spirit to pray and seek God's will for each 'moment' of each day. It is our "heart" that determines how we respond. Seems many of our choices are as follows:

Do as little as possible VS Giving full attention to details!

Showing UP VS Running Away

Doing things halfway VS Finishing the Job

Giving Up VS Staying the course

Quitting VS Beginning Again

Discouraged VS Encouraged

Despair VS Hope

Saddened VS Joyful

Looking Inward VS Looking Outward

Lies VS Truths

Lost VS Found

Fear VS Faith

Isolating VS Duty and Responsibility

Useless Vessels VS Vessels of Honor

Looking out For Oneself VS Caring for Others

Spiritually Blind VS Spiritual Alive

Careless VS Careful

"If you take 'time' for prayer, you will have a real living God, and if you have a **'living' God,** you will have a radiant life." Dr. R. A. Torrey

O PRAISE THE NAME OF THE LORD our GOD

I cast my mind to Calvary.
Where Jesus bled and died for me.
I see His wounds, His hands, His feet.
My Savior on that cursed tree.

His body bound and drenched in tears.
They laid Him down in Joseph's tomb.
The entrance sealed by heavy stone.

Messiah **STILL** and all alone.
Then on the third at break of dawn,
The son of heaven rose again.
O trampled death where is your sting?

He shall return in robes of white.
The blazing son shall pierce the night.
And I will rise among the saints.
My gaze transfixed on Jesus's face.

O praise the name of the Lord our God
O praise His name forever more
For endless days we will sing your praise
O Lord, oh Lord our God!

Hillsong
Writers: Martin w. Sampson, Benjamin William Hasting, Dean Michael Ussher

Epilogue

"Still" was uploaded, and a draft copy was ordered from Ingram Publishing. The day the UPS driver arrived to deliver the draft copy, he stopped first at my sister's home next door. I drove over to my sister's at the exact time the UPS driver got back into his truck. I parked my vehicle in the top parking area and I got out to make my own delivery to my sister. The driver drove up to me and stopped and said, "I have a package for you as well!" I replied, "Hand it to me right here, it will save you the stop!" He pulled out a small box and handed it to me. I exclaimed, "I know exactly what this is – it is the draft of my book "Still"!" He said, "Really!" I replied, "Yes, wait - I'll show you!" I opened the box and pulled out the book and showed him the front and the back cover with the picture of me wearing one of the hats from London. I said, "I should have been in London when my husband had his stroke on a missionary trip!" He replied, 'You gave me one of your books before and I read and liked it!" I replied, "I will gift you 'Still' as well!" He left and I went on my way.

The very next day, I learned that my friend Caroline DeLoreto was in the ICU at UVM Medical Center. Her birthday present was in a beautiful box on my kitchen table. It was Sunday, so after church service, I drove to the UVM Medical Center to deliver her birthday gift as well as her husband's birthday gift (their birthdays are one week apart). I rarely shop on Sunday, but this day would be different. I stopped at the grocery store to purchase 'chocolates' to gift to the staff of the ICU. That morning, I would wear the London hat featured on the back of this book! When I arrived, Caroline was having tests done, and I was told to wait in the ICU waiting room, the very same place we had waited for word on Fabien's triple bypass heart surgery. Adam Taft texted me that he, Carmilla, and one of my sisters were in the cafeteria and invited me to join them. I went to put the box and the grocery bag full of chocolate on the counter next to the kitchen in the waiting area. I interrupted a family's conversation to ask if it was okay for me to leave my gift box and bag on the counter. An older man said, "Go ahead it will be safe." I proceeded to leave, when this older man said, "And I really like your hat!" I turned around to bring him the gift pack with the Statue of Liberty and said, "I am visiting my friend who is from England and I dressed to brighten his day; his wife Caroline is in ICU. He then told me, "My wife is in the ICU and I am amazed to meet a fellow believer here. I am a missionary and pastor!" I said, "I have several faith-based books with true accounts of the power of the Lord to take 'ordinary things' and make them quite extraordinary!" He introduced me to his family. Then, one of his sons in the room said, "I know who you are! You have a book called, "Still" This shocked me! I replied, "How do you know that?! No one knows about this book yet?!" He replied, "My best friend is the UPS driver that delivered that book to you yesterday and he told me all about you and about that hat!"

The 'occurrence' reminded me of a very similar experience when cups were given to me by my very good friend, that ended up on the cover of my 2nd book, "Experiencing God's Amazing Ways". When I shared with this friend this account of being recognized in the ICU Waiting room for this book, she told me to add this as an Epilogue! So here it is for your own pondering! The statistical probability factor makes my own mind spin! I had not wanted to wear the 'hat' but felt 'compelled to do so!

Another odd event happened when I finished "The Trueman Bryer Memory Book". My friend Sue gifted me an old book by Reverand Daniel March entitled "Night Scenes in the Bible" just the day before I went to care for my friend Trueman in his home. The next morning, I randomly opened to page 255, exactly where a description of a 'true man' was included! Excerpts from the chapter "A night storm on the sea" are below (some of which are included within the commentary at the end of Trueman's book):

"When the disciples saw Jesus walking upon the waves, they thought they saw a spirit, an unreal and ghostly shadow, appearing to terrify rather than to comfort and deliver them. And yet he was the most true and real man that ever walked the earth. In him the troubled, longing weary soul finds the only reality which satisfies its great want. He is more real, true and satisfying to the earnest, thinking aspiring mind than wealth or learning or pleasure or power. His grand purpose in all his instructions is to make us true men – not angels, but beings not destitute of any of the passions, appetites, affections that are essential to our humanity: he would make us true men. This it is to be a Christian; this it is to be a follower of Christ; this it is to receive Christ to the heart. He is to be a <u>true</u> <u>man</u>. To be a Christian it is only necessary to be a <u>true</u> <u>man</u> – to love, believe and obey the truth. No man can think of a more desirable close of life for himself tan that he

may be found faithful to his convictions, true to his own deepest sense of obligation."

Obedience to the leading of the Lord from our 'heart' produces 'extremely rare events'. We are assured that 'in Him we live and move and have our being. He is the vine and we are the branches and without Him we can do nothing! (Acts 17:28; John 15:5)

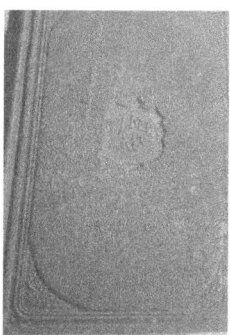

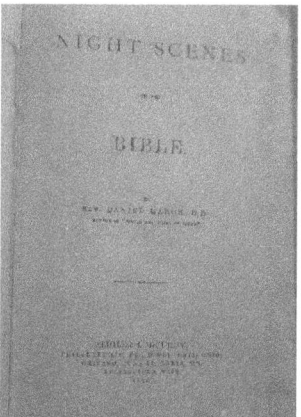

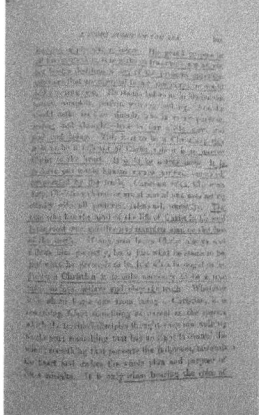

BOOKS BY DAWN DENSMORE-PARENT:

"DIVINE ENCOUNTERS: The Reality of God, Angels, and Demons" This book provides unique and captivating accounts of God's extraordinary ways, including allowing individuals to appear after they die. Her journey will make you laugh as well as cry, as you see how God can use anything, even hippopotamuses to show his love.

"For Such a Time as This?" Mordecai asked Esther, "Who knoweth whether thou art come to the kingdom for such a time as this?" (Esther 4:14). My question is: "Are we, Christians, alive on earth now (as Esther was then), 'For Such a Time as This?"

"Experiencing God's Amazing Ways" This book contains many unexpected events that defy explanation. It truly is the power of God's Holy Spirit that allows us to experience the presence of the Lord daily in our life – right now!

"Experiencing God's Priceless, Precious Promises" Life's challenges offer us opportunities to be 'thankful' for all things in our life. For I know the thoughts that I think toward you, saith the Lord, thoughts of peace, and not of evil, to give you an expected end (Jeremiah 29:11).

"The truth shall set you free: The Prison Letters". This book contains 52 letters written in 2020 of extraordinary events! These 'letters' contain the daily adventures of living with Fabien.

"The "True Man" Memory Book" as told to Dawn Densmore-Parent, by Trueman Bryer contains memories from Trueman of his childhood, growing up, along with his marriage and amazing children. "But seek ye first the Kingdom of God and His Righteousness and all these things shall be added unto you" (Matthew 6:33).

"The Incredible Life of a French Gypsy" as told to Dawn Densmore-Parent by Claude D. "Frenchy" Mongeau, known as a French Gypsy, traveled the world. This account of 'true love' warms the heart!

www.ingramcontent.com/pod-product-compliance
Lightning Source LLC
Chambersburg PA
CBHW042337040426
42446CB00021B/3476